I0116032

Dr. Beena A. Mahida

Teaching Short Stories

Publish World

2015

Teaching Short Stories

Dr. Beena A. Mahida

Publish World

2015

Price : $7.86

First Edition : April, 2015

ISBN : 978-1-988004-02-0

ISBN Allotment Agency : Library and Archives Canada (Govt. of Canada)

Published & Printed by
Publish World
81, Woodlot Crescent,
Etobicoke,
Toronto, Ontario, Canada.
Postal Code- M9W 6T3
Phone- +1 (647) 633 9712
http://www.canadapublish.com

Center at India :
Publish World,
Near Nandbhumi, A-V Road, Anand, Gujarat (India)
http://www.publishworld.org

PREFACE

Short story is one of the most popular forms of literature in modern time. It has now asserted its place as a distinct art form. It is the oldest form of literature. People are telling and hearing them from generation to generation. Children and grown up, all alike are charmed by it. Stories have been told in every country from time immemorial and each country has accumulated a rich store of tales. In the hands of modern writer it has become a perfect work of art.

As a distinct literary form, it is of recent origin but as a piece of tale, it is almost as old as man himself. The love of story is ingrained in us. Children and grown up all alike, are charmed by it. It fulfills two of the strongest human instincts. The desire to amuse & the desire to teach. It must have existed for thousands of years before the art of writing was known to the world. It began very early in human history when, perhaps, our primitive ancestors getting bored with the straggle of daily life must have released himself by narrating a tale to him companions. The instinct to listen to stories is deeply rooted in human mind. People are telling and hearing then from generation to generation and each country has accumulated a wide store of tales.

A Student of Literature cannot start his study-journey of literature without this popular literary genre. The book starts with origin, development and form/elements of short story. I have also included analysis and summary of world's best short stories like 'The Last Leaf', 'Son and Moon', 'Mr. Know All' and Many More which are taught in major institutes where literature is taught. It is followed by Questions & Answers Section. I have tried my level best to analyze every aspects of Short Stories.

Wish you a Joyful Reading....!

- Dr. Beena A. Mahida

CONTENTS

ORIGIN AND DEVELOPMENT OF SHORT STORY

Literature has various forms like poetry, drama novel, short story, etc. In modern time, the short story has emerged as one of the popular forms of literature.

THE ORIGIN OF THE SHORT STORY

As a distinct literary form, it is of recent origin but as a piece of tale, it is almost as old as man himself. The love of story is ingrained in us. Children and grown up all alike, are charmed by it. It fulfills two of the strongest human instincts. The desire to amuse & the desire to teach. It must have existed for thousands of years before the art of writing was known to the world. It began very early in human history when, perhaps, our primitive ancestors getting bored with the straggle of daily life must have released himself by narrating a tale to him companions. The instinct to listen to stories is deeply rooted in human mind. People are telling and hearing then from generation to generation and each country has accumulated a wide store of tales. These stories are of varied type's simple comical, serious, realistic and wonderful. So it has its beginning in folk life.

The custom of narrating tales in the ancient ages was popular both in the East and West A.C. ward is of opinion that Jesus Christ was the originator of the short story. Like all early literature the

Gopel were transmitted orally, It was meant for spiritual enlighten it yet had perfection of the form. Some of the earliest stories are found in the Vedas and in the Upanishads, in the old Testament. in the Buddhist, Jatakas, in Panchtrantra, and the fables of Aesop.

In England the short story enjoyed popularity in the Middle Ages. In the 14th C$_0$. Chaucer wrote. "The Canterbury Tales in the Elizabethanage Greene, Lodge and Nashe wrote some stories but it lacked unity. The only writer of worthy of attention is Thomas Deloney wrote. The Gentle craft". In the 17^{th}C$_0$ Bunyan, Defoe and swift wrote longer tales. The 18th c. also made no notable progress in the art of the short story. Steele, Addison, Goldsmith wrote a tale of morality.

The short story has its origin in the 19th c. It began in America in 1830, The principles of the modern story were first of all formulated by Nathaniel Hawthorne and Edgar Allan Poe. Both laid stress on the singleness of effect" as the hall mark of good story. In 1865 Rudyard Kipling had in produced the story as an independent literary form to the English people.

In America, Washington Jrving, Fitz. James, Bret Harte, O Henry, Stephan crone, Anderson, Faulkner. exercised a great influence on short story. In Russian, Gorgi, Dostoevsky, Tolstoy, and chekov, exercised the deepest influence on the development of modern story. In France, Maupassant, Balzac, also produced greatest Shorty. By the year 1860 the Russian, the American

French short story had developed into an appreciable limit, but in England it developed very slowly.

Setting : If refers to the Time, Place and mood of the story :

Time : It refers to the time like the morming, Evening afternoon setting of the story. If is also applied to the ancient era or the modern background of the story.

Place : It refers to the description of the place where action the story takes place. It may be the village or the town or city so it refers to the urban or rustic setting of the story.

Mood : This aspect of the story present the emotional aspect of the story. The mood of the story may be pathetic, ironical satirical, humorous, social, fantastic, etc.

FORM OF SHORT STORY

Short story is one of the most popular forms of literature in modern time. It has now asserted its place as a distinct art form. It is the oldest form of literature. People are telling and hearing them from generation to generation. Children and grown up, all alike are charmed by it. Stories have been told in every country from time immemorial and each country has accumulated a rich store of tales. In the hands of modern writer it has become a perfect work of art.

It is favored by many distinguished (popular) fiction writer but as a form it has been neglected so it is rather difficult to attempt a comprehensive definition of this form. The short story has never been adequately defied. Each one has tried to define it in his own way.

DEFINITIONS OF SHORT STORY :

Generally, speaking a short story is a story which is very short, Some people consider it as an expression of life. Others describe it as the recital of events H.G.Wells, the writer of Scientific fiction defines it "as The jolly art of making something bright and moving, it may be pathetic or humourous, horrified or illuminating and it takes 15 to 50 minutes to read. H.E. Bates says" It has something of the indefinite and infinite variable nature of a cloud" Ellery sedge wick holds that" a short story is like a horse race. It is the start and the finish that count most."

Chekhov, the Russian novelist calls it "As a slice of Life."

In short, it is said that short story is a kind of prose fictions prose narrative, usually more compact and intense than the novel and novelette.

THE LENGTH OF SHORT STORY

The short story is characterized by brevity. So it is necessary that its subject should be of a nature that can be effectively developed within the prescribed limits. Absolute economy of means is to be used and everything superfluous is to be strictly avoided.

There are several arguments about the length of the story. Some people believe that it should be completed (read) at a single sitting. Some say that it should run into several hundred lines or words others say that it may run into several pages. Henry James, the American novelist opined that there should be Six or eight thousand words.

Somerset Mangham believes that there should be 1600 or 2000 words. But a Genre cannot be arithmetical defined.

The length of the story cannot be decided by words or pages. A short story must be a narrative of considerable length, not too short, not too long. It is the impact of the story which is more important than the length of it. The story should have a moderate length.

Following are the chief elements of short story.

INCIDENT

The range of the short story in respect of the incident (theme) is practically unlimited. Every subject between heaven and Earth is fit for the short story generally; the incident of the story is taken from life. Life is abundantly rich to provide raw material to the writer. The writer of a short story selects significant details from life and adds flesh and blood to the skeleton of the story. Story is a sensitive writer's response to what is going on around him. The writer finds some secret of life in his experience and he reveals this secret of life and makes our life worth living. A certain shape is given to it by his artistic skill.

The incident may be an Event or an Experience of the writer. The incident may be Real or imaginary. The Real incidents includes the contemporary problems of the society, world, & country as well as the human emotions and feelings like jealousy, hatred, sorrow, happiness, bliss, joy etc. The imaginary incident pertains to magic, a suspense and horror. Like "The Tales of 'Arbian Nights". They present unrealistic even improbable situation yet they are all convincing because it has the coherence of experience. In the modern story, it happens that the writer does not introduce any external events but only the inner working of mind, the technique called the stream of consciousness.

The conflict before the writer is how to select the incidents from life or society because many incidents inspire him. So the work of writer is difficult He should take up only that incident which gives pleasure as well as some moral lesson to the reader which are the aim of a short story.

PLOT

The plot can be considered as the backbone of a story. The plot means the entire sequence of events. The plot of the story should be simple. It should never be complex. The writer presents the problems of life. Though the problem may be complex or simple it should be capable of suggesting a solution. The character must be able to find ways to solve it. So the ending of a story reports the result of the character's final decision on how to solve the problem which may include a change in the major character. The reader should have been prepared for it from the beginning. But it does not mean that end should be foreseen. Many stories depend on the elements of shock, surprise and suspense to make the end effective. It is known as "Twist at the end stories". Writers like O' Henry and Guy De Maupassant are very well known for such kind of end in this story.

Though, the writer is free to use his own technique, yet there are certain rules which if he follows make his story appealing. The following elements he should remember for construction of the story.

EXPOSITION

It is the beginning of the story and it introduces the character and its motif directly or indirectly.

DEVELOPMENT OF ACTION

The characters start their actions and the events begin to take place and the plot gradually develops on logical lines.

CONFLICT

In the development of plot difficulties being to arise. Every story contains obvious conflict between characters, between two desires within a character and between a character and his society. This conflict is the core of the story's structure.

CLIMAX

The conflict leads to climax. The climax of the story is the moment at which the conflict is most intense and at which its outcome become inevitable.

DENOUEMENT

It refers to the end of the story. The complication that had arisen earlier are now solved. The mystery is explained. & the story comes to an end.

CHARACTER

The writer of a story should maintain an economy of characters like incidents. The writer cannot give details like a novel because the scope of a short story is limited. It does not offer a wide canvass of life. So it looks like a beautiful picture on a small canvass.

Usually short story presents one or two characters. If there are many characters, many incidents will take place and all these incidents together will not be able to reveal the single secret of life. The novel portrays life on a broader canvas and the novelist aims at representing a larger period or the whole life of a character, whereas the short story writer deals with a fragment of life, or only one phase of life and for that the writer needs only one or few characters.

The character in the story always faces a problem of life and he finds solution sometime consciously or unconsciously. Everything that happens in the story comes to the reader through his senses. The character holds the story together. When the reader identifies himself emotionally and intellectually with the character, then the story is completely believable and capable of being experienced. Because, the writer gives some governing characteristic to the character like jealous nature, cruelty; loving, kind, innocent, benevolent, etc. and these characteristics may be altered by event or affected. Yet the action and decisions of the character to be believable and it must correspond to what a reader knows of his total personality. The character displays in the scene by his action and speech and thoughts. He is identified by a physical characteristic like face, gait, tone, size, age etc. which clearly identifies him. In the stories of "Panchrtrant" animals perform the role of character. But they are an allegorical representation of the weaknesses and strength of human beings.

Sometimes, the writer also introduces minor characters who help the main character to develop within a story. They possess a distinguish characteristic. They may add humour or reality in a story. But they hardly appear in a short story unless they serve a specific function.

DIALOGUE – DICTION

The language of the short story is characterized by economy. The short story aims at economy of phrasing and singleness of effect and so diction have taken a new importance for story writer. Every word in it should have its own importance. Dialogues are necessary in drama or in one act play but story writer can use dialogue for the introduction of subject &character.

STYLE – DESCRIPTION OR NARRATION

The writer presents his story through description or narration. Through description the writer creates an atmosphere, or suggests the future course of action. But he does not give the details like in a novel. Sometimes the writer through narration presents the story. He himself directly talks with the reader and he himself becomes one of the important characters.

THE CASTAWAY

- Rabindranath Tagore

Rabindranath Tagore (1861-1941) was a Bengali poet, philosopher, artist, playwright, composer and novelist. India's first Nobel laureate, Tagore won the 1913 Nobel Prize for Literature. He composed the text of both India's and Bangladesh's respective national anthems. Tagore travelled widely and was friends with many notable 20th century figures such as William Butler Yeats, H.G. Wells, Ezra Pound, and Albert Einstein.

SUMMARY

At chandernagore, because of storm, and ship wreck Nilkanta happened to arrive at the riverside villa where Kiran, a generous lady is staying with her husband in order to recover from her illness. Kiran becomes happy. His arrival was an accident. Nilkanta was a Brahmin boy and belonged to a theatrical troupe. Within a short time he became one of the members of Kirans' family. He was happy with his new life as he considered it as a double escape from his cruel master and other world. With his mixing nature he became friendly with the villagers and even with the mongrel village dogs. Kiran was taking care of him. She provided him new clothes and gradually attached to him He also used to make her happy by performing different roles during the afternoon time. But of course Kiran's husband Sharat and her mother in law disliked Nilkanta for his ill manners. Sometime Sharat beat him but compared to Nilkantas' former life it was nothing so he bear it. He also tried to learn reading & writing. He

was attached too much with Kiran and the house that he just forgot that he was a destitute little slave of the theatrical troupe.

But the comfortable life of Nilkanta was changed with the arrival of Satish, the younger brother of Sharat. Kiran found a new company as she was the same age of Satish. Their time passed in games, quarrels laughter etc. Nilkanta felt that he was neglected by her. For that he considered Satish as responsible man. His heart was filled up with bitterness & anger for him. He was helpless and used to show his anger on his friends and pet morgrel dogs. Formerly, Kiran used to serve him food and used to sit with him while he was eating. Whereas after Satish's arrival She did not find time for him. Nilkanta was deeply hurt and sometimes refused to eat with a hope that his refusal would reach to Kiran and she would come. But Kiran never came as per his desires. He wept during the time of night but no general hand of Kiran soothed him. He was a Brahain so he cursed Satish and thought that it would never go in vain because he had no courage to show his jealousy and enmity to Satish. Nilkanta was grown up without the love of anyone as he was orphan. He yearned for love and fortunately Kiran showered her love over him. So now he could not tolerate her love shared for Satish. He found Satish as rival and developed jealousy for him. Inspite of her willingness Kiran was unable to take him to her native and when he realized that he would have to separate, he became restless.

In his restless mood, in our week moment of life he stole the favorite ink stand of Satish. In the house ever one suspected him as a thief except Kiran. She had great faith in him and so she couldn't imagine him even in a dream as a thief. But she was wrong because when she opened his bag to place the parting gift for him she found the ink. stand. She was shocked as Nilkanta had betrayed her. Nilkanta knew that he would never convince her that he was not a thief but out of jealousy he had done this wrong deed. Too much love for Kiran made him to steal. He felt ashamed that in the eye of his god mother he proved do be thief who loved him. With despair, he left the house and Kiran without giving any explanation and became a castaway forever.

Indeed, Nilkanta touches the heart of the readers with his deep love for his god mother Kiran. His feelingsfor her can't be understood by anyone but ouly she is capable of understanding his feelings. We feel sorry for him at the end. His anger and jealousy for Satish are so much that he steals his ink stand yet we can't lable him as a thief as we know his emotion. But for Kiran he proves a thief which is unbearable for him as he has betrayed the faith of her.

QUESTIONS & ANSWERS

(1) Discuss the Character of Kiran.

Tagore's "The castaway" is a heart touching story for its character and the treatment of the subject matter. The two characters Kiran and Nilkanta move the heart of the readers. It is a story of innocent love between kiran and Nilkanta.

Kiran was a young woman with gentle and kind heart, She became seriously ill. In her village she was loved and liked by all. So the villagers become anxious at her illness. Her husband Sharat was worried about her illness and thought that the change of air might recover her so they came to Chandernagore for a change of air she started recovering but yet she looked pale and weak.

Kiran was fed up with her life at chandernagore because she felt very lonely there. She was a social woman and here she was also fed up with medicine and dieting. So she wanted to go back to her home as early as possible. But Sharat wanted to stay at chanderanagore till Kiran, recovered completely. This shows that Kiran likes the society and the company of human beings.

Her life at chandernagera at last becomes cheerful when Nilkanta, a Brahmin boy arrived at her home Being a woman of helping nature she took a great care of this castaway boy. Her love and care make Nilkanta felt that he belonged to this family and not to the theatrical troupe. In return, Nilkanta also makes her happy by performing different roles at the noon time. He become the pet of Kiran and she forgets her desire to go back to her home Her cheerful and lovely nature was also evident in her relation with her brother in law Satish. So she spreads happiness and pleasure in the life of everyone whom she meets. But her attachment and concern for Satish arose jealousy in the heart of Nilkanta. He felt ignored and neglected. He considered Satish as his rival for Kirans love But Kiran was not aware about the mental condition of Nilkanta. It was only when Nilkanta wept at the mention that he would have to go back to his village, as she could not take him with her she realized that she had created a tie of affection which Nilkanta was not ready to break.

She was hurt when Nilkanta was accused as a thief of Satish's ink. Stand. She was not ready to consider him as a thief. She had faith and trust on him. But she was disillusiaoued when in order to place a parting gift for Nilkant, she opened his bag. She found Satish's ink stand. in his bag. She was shocked, & puzzled she thought that she was betrayed by Nilkanta. Nilkanta had btrayed her trust. She was so much hurt by this incident that Tagore very touchingly presents the state of her mind" Nilkanta also felt ashamed before her as he store it only out of jealousy.But without explaining it he left her forever with sad heart. Kiran threw the bag in the river so that no one could consider Nilkanta as a thief. This behavior of Kiran shows that she tried to protect Nilkanta even when she found him to be a thief.

Indeed, Kiran in the story "The castaway" proves to be a god mother of Nilkanta. Only she is capable of understanding the emotions and mind of Nilkanta as she is sensitive lady. She showers such a motherly affection over the castaway boy that he cannot imagine his existence without her. Her lovely nature makes Nilkanta to forget his own identify. But at the end she is disillusioned as the boy whom she trusted & loved prove unfaithful Kiran with her sensitivity, helping nature, leave a lasting impression on the mind of the reader.

HALF A RUPEE WORTH

- R.K.Narayan

R. K. Narayan is among the best known and most widely read Indian novelists writing in English. In addition to his novels, Narayan has authored five collections of short stories, including **A Horse and Two Goats**, **Malguidi Days**, and **Under the Banyan Tree**, two travel books, two volumes of essays, a volume of memoirs, and the re-told legends **Gods, Demons and Others**, **The Ramayana**, and the **Mahabharata**. He wrote fourteen novels, five volumes of short stories, a number of travelogues and collections of non-fiction, condensed versions of Indian epics in English, and the memoir **My Days**.

SUMMARY

Half a Rupee worth is an interesting story by R.K. Narayan. Here he has described one eccentric character and his love for money Subbiah is the main character of the story. He was a grain merchant who was obsessed with the idea of making immense profit out of his sales of rice. The chief merchandise in his shop was rice. Subbiah wanted to make wealth as a dealer of rice only.

In the beginning of the story, we are informed what he stocked all varieties of rice from the cheapest quality to the finest type. Though his shop was dingy and congested, it was a heaven-like place for him. His business flourished continually. He was so skillful that during periods of drought (famine) he labored and acquired rice to earn profit. When harvest was plentiful, he would not stock much rice as there were slim chances of earning huge profit. He always intended to exploit the opportunity. He never thought of his duty towards humanity. He concentrated on hoarding and black marketing. He reminds us the present day businessman who forget their social responsibility and rob our fellow citizens during scarcity of essential commodities like oil, sugar, kerosene etc.

The writer gives us an account of the shaping of the career of Subbiah. He takes us back to his boyhood when he was forced by his father to serve as shop assistant. He longed for freedom and enjoy sports and films but his father did not allow him this freedom. His father believed that a boy after ten should be horse whipped if he was to become the right person. His father practiced this Principle so rigorously that Subbiah saw noting but rice and thought nothing but the price and profit of grain.

After the death of his father Subbiah became the owner of the shop. In addition to the shop, Subbiah owned cows and buffalo. He was also a money lender. He lent money to desperate persons at exorbitant rates of interest which enabled him to acquire dozens of houses. This way, he resorted to unfair means to get money from all sources. He became immensely wealthy and displayed his wealth in the life style of his family members. His wife wore rich clothes and was loaded with gold ornaments. Their lavish life-style was revealed in the décor of his house also. He was very busy throughout the day.

But his life changed during the Second world war. At first he was frightened about this. But then he prospered because of war. During the world war saigen and Burma stopped exporting rice so in India there was a scarcity of rice. But in Subbiah's godown there was a huge stock of rice so he sold rice at exerbit. He was deft in measuring. He cheated people by weighing less quantity and collected considerable stock of rice.

Because of the scarcity the government imposed Food controlling. He found out a solution to take advantage of the situation and opened a fairprice Grain Depot. He accepted the rules of the rationing shop but as he was cunning he gave bribe to the officials who were in change of examining the stock. So he retained all the rice out of sight and out of paper.

One day one poor man came to him for rice. He has already closed his shop. That man had only half a rupee and he wanted to buy one sheer of rice. The official rate for rice was three sheers for a rupee. So he told the poor man that he could give him only half a sheer of rice for half a rupee. That man agreed and Subbiah asked him to wait for him in the street. Three hours passed but he did not return. So the poor man searched for him in the street. Then he went to Subbiah's house. Subbiah's wife was also very anxious. They went to his secret godown. Through ventilator they saw Subbiah's hand under the bags of rice. Subbiah was dead because the rice bags had fallen on him. He lost his life only for half a rupee. He was crushed beneath the heavy load of rice bags that fell on him while getting rice worth half a rupee.

Subbiah's character reminds us the character of Tolstoy's Pahom when we find in the story "How much land does a man need." Like pahom he was also greedy man and like him he met a tragic death. The theme of a story is poetic justice that virtue is rewarded and vice is punished.

QUESTIONS & ANSWERS

(1) What were the times like for a rice seller when there was a "depression in the trade"?

When the harvest was plentiful then the rice seller would not stock much rice as there were little chances of profit. When the harvest was plentiful there would not be scarcity of rice, so they could not sell it at exorbitant price. Rice would sell very cheaply everywhere. If they sold only rice all day and night they could earn only Rs.50/- at the end of month. This situation is known as a depression in the trade.

(2) How did Subbiah's father train him for his job?

During the time of subbiah's childhood his father forced him to assist him in his shop. So he served as a shop assistant to his father when he was child. At that time he wanted to wander in the crowded streets, he wanted to see cinemas, football matches and wrestling tournaments. But his father did not allow him this freedom. His father believed that a boy after ten years should be beatlike horse if he was to become a right person. He taught his theery so forcefully to the child that when Subbiah grew up he only thought of rice and spoke of rice.

(3) What did Subbiah spend some of his newly acquired wealth on?

Subbiah acquired wealth by unfair means. He spent it on his life tyle. He sent his children to the school and also bought brocaded cap and velvet coats for them and provided them a home tator. It was a custom in rich families to employ a teacher at home. His wife also ware heavy gold ornaments and silk sarees. He built two more storeys and several halls to his old house and painted all the walls with a blue oil paint and put pictures of Gods in gilt frames.

(4) Discuss Significance of the title of the story.

The title of the story "Half a rupee Worth" is very appropriate and also suggestive. The title evaluates the worth a life of man. If a man is excessively greedy and exploits, other human beings his life not worth living. This is indicated through the character of Subbiah who was very greedy man. He lived only for money. He was a grain merchant. He wanted to become a sole merchant of rice. He earned money by unfair means During the world war he opened a rationing shop and by giving bribe to the government officials he prospered. But he met with a tragic death. He could do anything for money. When he found half a rupee he agreed to give rice to the poor man. He wanted to get that half a rupee. But he was crushed under the bags of rice while getting rice worth half a rupee He lost his life only for a half a rupee. The title reflects that if a person's greed is boundless it ruins him. Thus, Subbiah's life is worth no more than half a rupee.

(5) How did Subbiah prosper in spite of the food control?

During the war there was a scarcity of rice so the government imposed food controlling. Subbiah was baffled and Worried and he raved against the government asking why should they indulge in their business. They should content themselves with tax collection, catching thieves and putting up drains. But he found out a solution and opened a fair price grain Depot (rationing shop). The scheme of the rationing shop appeared to him absurd yet he accepted its rules. He was very cunning and wanted to retain all the rice so he gave a lot of money to the officials and retained all the rice out of sight and out of paper. He was deft in weighing rice. He cheated customers by weighing less quantity and collected a considerable stock of rice. He was irregular in opening the Fair price Grain shop so people had to come to his shop several times. Again, when people had money he had no rice and when he had rice people had no money. He packed his godown with rice but declared that it contained paper and rags which he had stored to meet both the ends meet. He used to befool people by saying that he had no rice but if they paid in advance he would get it from someone. So by all this manipulation he prospered inspire of food controlling.

SPARROWS

- K. A. Abbas

K. A. Abbas was a master at short stories, presumably influenced by O. Henry; however he through his writings presented a different picture of India. Humanism being one of the main themes in his writings just like Mulk Raj Anand. They both were contemporary writers of that India when our stories were cast on Black and White screen. Reading K.A. Abbas means a lot of historical and cultural throwback for the new generations.

SUMMARY

"Sparrows" is an excellent story by K. A. Abbas, In sparrows he depicted one character whose ambitions were crushed by his parents and the society and therefore he becomes a misanthrope. But when he was forsaken by the family and the society he relearned to love the world. The "sparrow" depicts the Re-trans formation of a middle aged man rather too late in life into tender hearted being.

Rahimkhan, the main character of the story was fifty years old farmer. In his village he was regarded by everyone as a cruel person. This is revealed through the talk of the villagers. One day

24

when the returned from the fields he learnt that his wife had run away from the house. He had two sons named Bundu and Nuru. But the eldest Bundu had run away from the house because of Rahimkhan's cruelty towards him and the younger son Naru also followed him and run away from the house. Then after he always felt that his wife also would run away from the house. So he did not feel surprise when she left him. His wife and his sons left him because he misbehaved with them He treated them with cruelty and never loved them as his own family. He was not a cruel man when he was young.

As a Youngman he was very cheerful and versatile man. He was a good athlete and no one could defeat him in kabadi and in wrestling. He fell in love with one Hindu girl named Radha, the daughter of Ramcharan. One touring circus came to his village. He wanted to join the circus because he loved adventure and travelling. But his father believed that to work in a circus was immoral work for a respectable person. His father and his ancestors were farmers so he should also work as a farmer. He wanted to marry Radha but the very idea of marrying a Hindu girl was infamous and irreligious. It would shock the conservative Muslims and Hindus. He wanted to reveal his feelings and thought of rebellion but he did not have enough courage to challenge the paternal authority or the social tradition. So both his ambitions in life were killed by his parents and social customs. He always felt that they were responsible for his failure in life and to take revenge against the society he became a misanthrope and treated his family very cruelly. No one could understood why he turned into a cruel man from once a cheerful man.

He treated his wife as a slave and he beat her everyday. She was used to it. If he did not beat her for a week, she feel strange. But now there was none in the house to whom he could show his anger. He did not feel sorry for it but only uncomfortable. Next day he got up very late and when he sat for smoke he found a nest of sparrows in the thatched roof. He peeped into it and found two baby sparrows only one day old. But their parents attacked him and Rahimkhan was surprised by the sparrows' effort to save their home and children Everyday he looked at the nest with interest. The two baby sparrows grew up and Rahimkhan developed intimacy with them and he called them Bandu and Naru the names of his own sons who he had not seen for several years. The four sparrows become his fast friends in the world.

His behavior also changed with the passing of the time. His neighbors' were surprised by his new behavior and saw it with suspicion. One day during monsoon when Rahimkhan returned from the fields he did not find sparrows in his hut. He saw into the nest found the four sparrows sitting in a nest huddled up within their feathers. The roof was leaking. Rahimkhan repaired the roof in heavy rain and became ill. But in the house there was no one to take care for him. The village people could not find him in the fields so they went to his house and found him talking. He was talking with the sparrows. He told them - "O Bandu, O Naru, who will feed you when I am gone" The people thought that he had become mad and informed his wife. She returned with her sons but the doors of the house were closed. They broke the doors and found Rahimkhan dead.

Thus, a man who is cruel becomes kindhearted but too late in his life. The author has shown how Rahimkhan once a cruel man is transformed into a loving and kindhearted man. It is the absence of love and warmth that makes him understand what love is

Sparrows gives us an excellent insight into the human mind. If a human being is deprived of love and tenderness, some frustrated persons divert their attention to sublime work and becomes a painter or sculptor (creative) There is also a possibility of such frustrated person developing bitterness or hostility against the society. Rahimkhan, who was deprived of his ambitions by social and religious factors reacted bitterly for him his bride was a symbolic gift of persecution by family and society.

(1) For thirty years from the time of his marriage Rahimkhan ill-treated his family, his bullocks and his neighbors. In what way did he do that and why?

When Rahimkhan was a Youngman he was a cheerful person and wanted to do something in his life. He cherished two dreams: to marry Radha and to join the circus. But his dreams were shattered by his family, and the society. He became misanthrope. Rahimkhan who was deprived of his ambition by society and religious factors reacted bitterly. He treated his wife as a slave and to take revenge against the family and society became a cruel person.

Sparrow is a short social story. The story is a comment on the paternal authority and social traditions. It tells how a young Rahimkhan is dented a career after his waort and a marriage with a girl of his wont by the strict paternal authority and social radiation.

For him his pride was a symbolic gift of persecution by his family and the society. He used to beat her everyday and therefore if he did not beat her she would feel strange. His wife had been both the symbol and target of all his grievances against family, society and life. So when she left him he did not feel sorry but only uncomfortable as if a necessary piece of furniture had been removed. He never loved his children as his own sons. He used to beat them severely and as a result they ran away from the house. His family had left him because of his ill treatment of them. He never loved his bullocks who were very useful to him in his farm, and beat them cruelly.

His neighbors also did not like his ride behavior. When they gathered for the evening soke they talked about his crucially Kelly considered him as a hard hearted devil. The sweet seller said that he was going worse and worse everyday because he beat poor Ramvo's child for only a trivial subject Ramnath the zaildar also said that Rahimkhan very cruelly beat his mare because she was wandering in his field. The old Patel said that he had never seen such a cruel person in his life and therefore there was no surprise what his two sons had left him. His neighbors did not like his behavior and were frightened of him. If he came near them they will stop talking.

Because of his frustration in life he treated his wife, children and neighbors very cruelly for thirty long years.

THE SILVER LINING

- Chaman Nahal

Chaman Nahal, also known as *Chaman Nahal Azadi*, is an Indian born writer of English literature. He is widely considered as one of the best exponents of Indian writing in English and is known for his work, *Azadi*, which is set on India's Independence and her partition. **Chaman Nahal received Sahitya Akademi Award for Azadi in 1977.**

SUMMARY

The Silver Lining is one of the interesting stories by Chaman Nahal. "The silver Lining" describes the agony of the parents of a handicapped child and how a guest who is similarly handicapped brings joy into the child's life.

The narrator of the story Mr. Dhanda Describes one of the pleasant experiences he had when he visited a private guest house in one of the hill resorts. The host and hostess were very kind to him and offered him a warm welcome. Mrs. Bhandari, the hostess belonged to South India yet she married Mr. Bhandari a north

Indian. But Mr. Bhandari was not rough man like most of the northern persons but a well mannered man. They had one daughter named promoting who was eight years old. Mr. Dhanda was attracted towards her because of her innocent look. He did not know the fact that she was leaf and dumb. When he called her she run away from the room and the Bhandaris told him that their daughter could not hear or speak. Mr. Dhanda was shocked to hear this Mr. & Mrs. Bhandari informed him that every time this situation arose when a new guest visited their guest house. They became friendly with her but soon realized that she was deal and dumb. This realization turned into a long discussion with every guest. Everytime the guest asked many questions like how this calamity had come down to her, whether it was from birth, whether anyone in the family suffered from the same misfortune, and what treatment was being given to her. All the time the parents answered the questions with hesitation and unwillingness.

Therefore Mr. Dhanda thought to save little promodni from this humiliating situation. He found out one solution and suggested to the Bhandaris. He suggested that they should prepare one chit and in that chit they should mention the following thing: "our daughter is deaf and dumb. You may hurt her by trying to be friendly too soon, as she can neither understand nor reply to your kind words you are requested to please give her time to approach you and make your acquaintance. Thank you." This chit should be circulated among the new visitors in a sealed cover. But it was opposed by Mrs. Bhandari because she thought that it was against her hospitality. But finally she agreed and this method worked very well. They were happy.

But one day one young man visited the guest house. He was twenty five years old. His name was Mr. David. Inspite of his long journey he looked very cheerful, but his nature was very strange. Mr. & Mrs. Bhandari were surprised by his arrogance and strange behavior because when Mrs. Bhandari asked him whether his journey was pleasant he only nodded his head when she asked him whether he would have coffee first or bath he only shrugged his shoulder. Mr. David found that sealed cover addressed to him, he read it and ran towards little promodni and Mrs. Bandari became angry as Mr. David had not followed the instruction of the chit. They run towards Mr. David but they found a totally different situation. Promodni was sitting in his lap and was laughing. They had never seen her laughing like this. They had not expected such situation. Mr. David revealed the secret that he himself was deaf and dumb. He also gave the information that there were training schools abroad for this type of children. He had received education in this type of school abroad. Now he was living a normal life like any human being. He wanted to start this type of training school in India also and he accepted Promodni as his first student. This unexpected incident brought joy in the life of the Bhandaris

QUESTIONS & ANSWERS

(1) What is the "Silver Lining" in the story? Do you consider it a suitable title?

The title "Silver Lining" has a reference to the popular adage (Maxim)" The darkest could has a silver lining." It encourages people who are in the grip of difficulties and misfortunes. The adage (proverb) teaches people not to be disheartened or dispirited by misfortunes because there was always a ray of hope likes a silver border to a dark cloud. The story is a good example of it. The handicapped child promodni who is deaf and dumb is in the grip of despair. Her parents, Mr. & Mrs. Bhandari are also distressed to see the condition of their daughter. The narrator, Mr. Dhanda, is also disturbed to see the handicapped girl. A chit is circulated to new guests so that the child may not be troubled emotionally. At this deepest moment of despair, Mr. David, a similarly handicapped man brings joy in the life of the despaired family. He informs them that there were schools for such handicapped children and training can make them live life in a perfectly normal manner. He himself, though deaf and dumb, was trained up in a school abroad. He wants to start one school for the handicapped so that they can live a very happy life. He also accepts promodni as his first student. This news brings happiness in the life of the family.The life of Bhandari family was surrounded by dark clouds of despair & depression. Mr. David's arrival brings a ray of hope or silver Lining in their gloomy life.

(2) The arrival of each new guest caused anguish to the Bhandari family. Describe the humiliation that the three of them suffered on such occasions.

The Bhandaris were the host and hostess of a private guest house. Their daughter promodni was leaf and lumb. In their guest house every time new visitors came for three or four days and developed friendship with promodni but soon they became aware of the fact that she was deal and dumb. and could not talk and hear them. They felt sympathy towards her and asked many questions to the parents about how this disaster had taken place, whether it was from birth, whether anyone in the family, suffered from this type of condition, what kind of treatment was being given to her. The Bhandaris gave the answers haltingly because those were agonizing moments to explain every time about their daughter's mistreated. The guests wanted to express sympathy on such occasions. The condition of promdni became worse as she knew that they were talking about her. So when the guests asked them about their daughter they felt humiliated.

(3) How did Mr. David bring happiness to the Bhandari family what future plans did he have for promodni?

The Bhandaris lived a life of disappointment and depression because of their daughters plight (miserable condition) she was deal and dumb and could not express all her feelings. She also lived in the world of despair. But her life changed when Mr. David arrived in their guest house. He brought happiness in the life of promodni. Like promodni he was also handicapped deal and dumb. But he did not dive in the world of despair. He interment them about the training schools for the handicapped By acquiring the training a handicapped person should live a normal life, like any other human being. He himself got training in one of the schools abroad. He could understand the sentences spoken by any person. He could read the lips and understood the meaning. His future plan was that he wanted to start one training school for the handicapped children, because in India these kind of schools were not developed much and all could not afford the expense of the training school abroad. He wanted to give useful service by starting of school and would admit promodni as his first students. This news brands joy in the life of the Bhandaris.

THE CURD SELLER

- Masti Venkatesa Iyengar

Maasthi Venkatesa Iyengar (6 June 1891 – 6 June 1986) was a well-known writer in Kannada language. He was the fourth among Kannada writers to be honored with the Jnanpith Award, the highest literary honor conferred in India.   He was popularly referred to as Maasti Kannadada Aasti which means Maasti is Kannada's Treasure. He is most renowned for his short stories. He wrote under the pen name Srinivasa. He was honoured with the title Rajasevasakta by then Maharaja of Mysore Nalvadi Krishnaraja Wadeyar.

SUMMARY

In this story the writer presents the problem of joint family system. The woman who was deserted by her husband at her young age, brought up her son alone. She wanted to govern the life of her own son even after he got married. This lead to a quarrel between the mother and her daughter in law.

Mangamma, an aged woman sold curds in the village. The narrator of the story, Ammayya usually took cards from her and was quite familiar with Managemma because she visited Ammayya when she went to the city and while coming back from the city after selling the curds. Mangamma often told her about her life and asked Ammayya about her life. Ammayya lived a happy life. Her husband deserted her when She was young, because she never kept herself look beautiful and her husband turned to another woman and left his wife and son. Now she was old and therefore from her experience she advised young Ammayya that she should be careful in her dressing. Mangamma also suggested to her four ways to keep the husband happy.

- A wife should prepare something nice for eating every day.
- A wife should dress well and look desirable whatever difficulty she finds at home.
- A wife should buy grocery herself without asking for it to her husband.
- A wife should keep some money with her and should give to her husband whenever he asks for it.

Mangamma believed that if a woman followed these things she should be happy throughout her life.

Mangamma often quarreled with her daughter in law only for trivial reasons. One day she informed Ammayya about this. When her daughter in law Nanjamma beat her little child, Mangamma objected to it and called her daughter in law that she was heartless. But Nanjamma thought what she had every right to bring order to her son. This small thing led to a big quarrel. Mangammia is son had taken the side of his wife and told her that his wife had every right to bring order to her son. His mother should not interfere her and also suggested to her she should live separately because she was not dependent on them.

Mangamma started living separately. Up to now she lived only for her son and grandson but she felt that she was neglected by them. She saved money for them up till now. She decided to spend the money for her own needs. She asked Ammayya about the cost of velvet jacket and also bought velvet jacket for her when her husband was with her she had never bought any good sari and now she became old and bought velvet jacket. The village people wondered when she wore it and ridiculed her. Her daughter in a law also commented about it. The quarrel between them went on like this.

Mangamma one day asked Ammayya to put her money into a bank because one man named Rangappa, a dandy and gambler wanted some money from Mangamma. Rangappa stopped her on her way to home and expressed . Sympathy for her condition but she did not give him any response. Next time when she met him he expressed his love but Managamma knew that he was treacherous and only wanted to please her to get money from her. Her grandson visited her so she was happy. He started living with her.

Nanjamma came there and threatened her son but he did not go with her. It created one problem for Managamma she could not take him to city when she went for selling curds. After sometime Nanjamma and her son came to her and requested her to return home she agreed and decided to hand over the curds selling business to Nanjamma.

Ammayya the narrator of the story also wanted to know the reaction of Nanjamma about her mother in law. Nanjamma told her that her mother in law insisted on having her own way. Insisted on having her own way in everything. But when she took objection when she beat her son she became angry. She wanted to govern her son's life because she was his mother not Mangamma when she heard that Rangappa wanted to get money from her mother in law. She made one plan she asked her son to go to his grandmother and stay with her. Her son did not stay with his grandmother willingly but his mother told him to do so. So that no one can take adventage of Mangamma situation and somekind of adjustment took place. The conflict was still goint on in the house.

The story of Managamma describes the sufferings of deserted woman and her love for her son. She was forsaken by her husband in her young age. At that time she sold cards and earned money for the house, and never dressed well but only thought how to keep the family. For that she had paid the penalty. Then after she diverted her attention in bringing up her child. She loved her son very much. But when he got married she expected that he should love her as before As she did not get love in young age she wanted love from her son. She did not tolerate that another woman her daughter in law could love her son more than she did. She could not understand the feelings of her daughter in law.

Mangamma did not want interference of her daughter in law. She wanted to run the life of her son, and grandson in her own way. This lead to a quarrel between them. They could not understand each other's feelings. Because of the idea of possession Mangamma suffered in her old age. From her young age to an old age she underwent many sufferings.

Thus, here the writer describes the old age conflict between mother in law and daughter in law in Indian joint family. This conflict is found in almost every home in India. The mother in law trying to dominate her son and the daughter in law trying to have upper hand in the struggle.

QUESTIONS & ANSWERS

(1) How did Mangamma close her husband ? What, according to her, are the different ways of keeping husbands true to their wives?

When Managamma was young she never dressed well. She never wore good sari and did not look pretly. She did not worry about looking beautiful and her husband was attracted towards another woman and deserted Magnamma. She also believed that she had committed crime by selling curds and milk. People believed that curds and milk should not be sold because they are Amrita. From her experience Managamma advised Ammayya that a wife should follow four ways if she wants to be happy through out in her life.

1. A wife should prepare something nice for eating everyday.
2. A wife should dress well and look desirable whatever difficulties she finds at home.
3. A wife should buy grocery herself without asking for it to her husband
4. A wife should keep some money with her and should give to her husband whenever he asks for it.

   According to Manganna any woman who follows these four ways would be happy in her life.

(2) Why did Nanjamma consider it necessary to bring Mangamma back to their house? How did she bring about the reconciliation?

Managamma lived separately from his son and grandson because of the quarrel among them. After sometime Nanjamma thought it was advisable to bring Managemma at home. They requested her to come back because Mangama was now old and she should take rest without wandering in the street in the hot sun. But this is not the feet. Mangamma had some money with her and one of the man of the village named Rangappa a dandy and gambler wanted some money from Mangamma. Nanjamma believed that her mother in law was willing to give him the money. Nanjamma did not tolerate that somebody could take her mother in law's money. She herself asked her son to go and stay with his grandmother. Her little child did not stay with his grandmother will evenly but his mother asked him. By doing this Nanjanna wanted to settle down the quarrel and bring Mangamma home.

(3) How did Nanjamma justify her behavior towards her mother in law?

Nanjamma informed Ammayya about her attitude towards her mother in law. Ammayya asked her why she had driven out her mother in law. Nanjamma told her that she did not want to behave rudely with her. But Mangamma wanted to dominate everything of the house. She wanted to ran the house in her own way. Mangamma did not want that her daughter in law should handle the things of the house. Mangamma never considered her son as the master of her house but behaved as if she was the mistress of the house. Nanjamma could not see this. She felt that her husband should be regarded as the master of the house yet she bore it but when Mangamma objected to her when she beat up her child she became angry. She believed that her mother in law should not interfere in her life. She had every right to run the life of her own son. mangamma should not object her.

(4) Discuss Character Sketch of Rahimkhan.

The story "sparrows" is a social story. It tells us how a cheerful and kind man is turned into a hard hearted cruel man because of strict and stern paternal authority and orthodox social customs. In the story Rahimkhan's dreams of life are destroyed. As his parents do not allow, he can not join the cirus as his career. As the social traditions come in the way he cannot marry a Hindu girl Radha. The result is that he becomes a hard hearted man.

Rahimkhan is about 50 yers old. He is strong and stout farmer. He is "Alone, Alone all Alone an the wide world". He has no relation with any one in the village people in the village hate him. He has ill nature. He beat a child for throwing a pebble at his oxen. He picks up quarrels with any one. He has no compassion for a child or a dumb animal. He is a married. But his wife and his two sons have left him because of his cruel beating. He is harsh with them because the world was harsh with him.

Rahimkhan was the best athlete in the village. He was expert in wrestling, kabbadi and swimming. He wanted to join a touring circus. In the circus he saw the career after his own heart He loved a Hindu girl named Radha. In her he found his soul mate. But his parents killed both ambitions. His father told him that circus work was low for a respectable farmer. He considered his idea for marrying Radha irreligious. He had no courage to rebel dry paternal authority and said Addison Radha married to a bunya and Rahimkhan also married. It was since then he has lived a life without love, feelings or enthusiasm an arranged marriage.

Rahim khan decided to avenge himself against his family and society. He regarded them responsible for his failure in life. (He takes the revenge of all on his wife an children. Beating his wife was become regular habit with him. The people did not understand him or sympathies with him. They showed utter indifference and hostility towards him. His wife tolerated all his cruelites with the slave like docility. This was his past.

But when they have left him. he feels lonely. He becomes a lonely soul . He does not feel unhappy because he has no love for his wife or children. He feels himself uncomfortable.

At the end he finds his friendship with the sparrows, which live in the nest in his hut. He has an attachment with the two baby sparrows. He calls them after the names of his lost sons. He becomes kind and loving. He loves them, take care of them and feels than. To protect them from the rain water, he repairs the leakage in the roof. He is drenched and gets fever. He dies with a worry who will feel the two little sparrows after his death. He does not die as a hard hearted man, he dies as a kind man me are happy that at the end he his changed into a kind man because of the sparrows. We sympathies with Rahim Khan because he becomes a victim of strict and rigid paternal authority and social traditions.

THE MARK OF VISHNU

- Khushwant Singh

Khushwant Singh was a reputed author with a wide collection of short stories, novels and literary treasures. s a writer, he was best known for his trenchant secularism,[2] humour, sarcasm and an abiding love of poetry. His comparisons of social and behavioural characteristics of Westerners and Indians are laced with acid wit.

SUMMARY

"The mark of Vishnu" is the story of a devotee of Vishnu whose blind reverence for a king cobra leads him to his death. Ganga Ram was an illiterate Brahmin and superstitious man. He was a servant. Since Ganga Ram was illiterate and superstitious the young boys in the house always mocked at him. Ganga Ram was devotee of Brahima, Vishnu and Shiva and regarded all the creatures sacred. The more dangerous the animal the more devoted Ganga Ram was and likewise he was devoted of Kala Nag who lived in the courtyard of the house.

He worshipped the Kala Nag but the young boys did not have any respect for Kala Nag. Ganga Ram used to offer milk to Kala Nag. Every night he put saucer full of Milk outside the hole near the wall and found it empty next morning. He believed that Kala Nag drank it but the boys meted at him by saying that it might be a cat who drank the milk But Ganga Ram was firm in his belief believed that the Kala Nag would not bite anyone as long as he offered him milk.

The boys could not agree with his foolish devotion for the cobra him because their science teacher told them that the Snakes did not drink milk and ate only once in several days. They informed him about the snakes which they had in their lab.

The boys told Ganga Ram that if they would see the Nag, they would kill him. But Ganga Ram replied that the Kala Nag has laid a hundred eggs and all would become cobras and there would be full of cobras in the house. The boys said that they would send them Bombay because they were useful for anti-snake bite serum and they would get money from it when Ganga Ram said that it was phanniyar and three hands long, the boys realized that Ganga Ram was liar because the phanniyar was the male and could not have laid eggs.

The boys were scientific in their approach towards Kala Nag. They liked Ganga Ram but they could not tolerate Ganga Ram superstitious nature. They cold not regard Kala Nag as the sacred creature. He was just a snake for them who was helpful in preparing anti snake bite serum. They wanted to change Ganga Rams attitude toward Kala Nag by informing him about its scientific use. But Ganga Ram stuck to his blind faith for Kala Nag.

QUESTIONS & ANSWERS

(1) How was the boys captured the kala nag and how did the kala nag escape?

In the "Mark of Vishnu" Khushwant singh depicted two types of person who were different in their attitude toward kala nag. Ganga Ram worshipped the kala nag who was living in the courtyard of house. But the boys in the house did not have respect for kala nag. Ganga Ram always protected the danger our animals. The boys could not harm them because of Ganga Ram. They wanted to see & cateh the kala nag and one day they saw the kalanag.

During monsoon they captured the kala nag. It rained heavily. The muddy ground was filled with worms, centypdes and velvety lady birds. All the holes were filled with water and the kala nag came out from the hole and sat on the lawn. For the first time the children had seen him, he was 6 feet long and they decided to catch him. Ganga Ram was fortunately not at home to save the live cobra. There was not any chance for the kala nag to escape because the ground was slippery and all the holes and gutters were full of water.

They surrounded the cobra with long bamboo sticks. The cobra became furious and tried to escape. He hissed and became red but the boys bit it in the middle and his back was broken. He could not move but the boys decided not to injure its hovel because they wanted to take him to their school and they put the cobra in a biscuit tin after, injuring it.

GOD SEES THE TRUTH, BUT WAITS

- Leo Tolstoy

Leo Tolstoyis best known for War and Peace (1869) and Anna Karenina (1877). He first achieved literary acclaim in his 20s with his semi-autobiographical trilogy, Childhood, Boyhood, and Youth (1852–1856), and Sevastopol Sketches (1855), based upon his experiences in the Crimean War. Tolstoy's fiction includes dozens of short stories and several novellas such as The Death of Ivan Ilyich, Family Happiness, and Hadji Murad. He also wrote plays and numerous philosophical essays.

SUMMARY

"God sees the truth, But waits" is an effective story by the famous Russian novelist Leo Tolstoy. The story is taken from his well known collection "Twenty Three Tales." This story is a tale of guilt and repentance. The story presents the sufferings of innocent man named Aksionov .

Aksionov (Ivan Dmitrich) is the main character of this story. Aksionov was a merchant and he was living in Vladimir. Once there was a fair in a distant town and Aksionov decided to go to the Nizhny fair and he got ready when he was going his wife told him that she had bad dream at night in which she saw that he would return home with grey hair i.e. as an old man. She requested him not to go but he ignored his wife's warning and set out for the fair. But he did not know the fact that he was leaving his family forever and henceforth he would live a life of sufferings.

On his way Aksionov met another merchant, whom he knew and they both stayed in one inn. They took tea together and then went to bed in adjoining rooms. Bat aksiovov got up early and left the inn. Hardly he had gone 25 miles, an official came there with two soldiers and they cross examined him. Aksionov was confused he did not know why he was being cross examined. The official cross examined him because the merchant with whom he had passed the night was murdered. They searched his luggage and got blood stained knife. Aksionov was found guilty Aksionov could not prove himself innocent and he was arrested for murdering the merchant and also for rubbing him off his 20,000 (twenty thousand) rubles. He was condemned to be flogged and sentenced to 26 years of imprisonment. His wife visited him in prison. Their children were very small. She informed him that she had sent a petition to the czar but it was rejected. She also suspected him and asked him if he had really committed the murder. It was very shocking for him because his own wife suspected him. Aksionov knew that only God know the truth. He had great faith in god He said "It is to him above we must appeal and from him above expect mercy" He knew that one day he would certainly got justice and he wrote no more petition and only prayed God. He was taken to Siberia.

Aksonov passed 26 years in prison in Siberia. He was totally changed. He became very serious and read the lives of saints and also got respect of the other prisoners. He was living an aim less life.

One day a new group of convicts came to the prison. Among them, there was one tall strong man of sixty. His name was Maker semyonich. With his conversation Akoionov knew that Maker was from Vladimir. It was Maker who had murdered the merchant and for which Aksionov was passing his life in prison. When Aksionov asked him it he knew the person who had killed the merchant. He replied that "must have been him in whose bag the knife was found and he also said. How any could put a knife into his bag while it was under his head. Aksionov realised that Maker was certainly the real convict and his heart was filled with revenge. He could not sleep. He felt that he was separated from his family and living this miserable life because of Makar. He longed for revenge. He passed for might but then he meditated and overcome his feeling of revenge.

One night Aksionov had seen Maker digging a hole to escape Makar threatened him that he would kill him if he revealed it to anyone. Aksionov replied that he had killed him long ago. He was not afraid of him. However the tunnel was found out. The governor came and asked all the prisoners and last came to Aksionov because he was honest man. But Akoiovov did not disclose

Makar's name so he did not take revenge even when it was possible.

Aksionov 's nobleness also enkindles Makar's heart and he also repented and he asked Alesionov to forgive him and also confessed his crine that he had really committed the murder and he was ready to declare that so that Akoionov would be released and could go to home. But it was too late Aksionov only said "God will forgive you." Aksionov did not want to go, he only waited for his death. Makar confessed his guilt but when Aksionov was released he had already left this world.

Thus, the story depicts how the kindness of Akoionov changed the heart of Makar. It is really said that forgiven is the best form of revenge". Aksionov was self sacrifice, kind hearted sympathetic and affectionate person. He feels compassion for the convict. He possessed the quality of forgiveness and nobleness. With this two qualities he transforms the Makar's heart (He has forgiven Makar's ingatitude fudge and saved him.

QUESTIONS & ANSWERS

(1) "Forgiveness is the best form of Revenge" – Discuss.

The story "God sees the truth, but waits" centers around this moral that forgiveness is the best form of Revenge. This moral is revealed through the character of Aksionor.

Man is not God, because he possesses both virtues and vices and the vices like Revenge, hatred, jealousy, Selfishness, envy, tempts man but when the man overcome these vices he comes nearer to God and the world remember them forever. Although they have to pass through many sufferings and miseries but their goodness, virtues inspire to earths. This story is a good example of above stated opinion.

Aksionov was a rich merchant and he was living a happy life with his family. One day He went to Nizny Fair and his visit to this fair bring brought misfortune in his life. He never returned to his home again. On his way he was arrested for killing the merchant with whom he stayed in the inn. He was arrested because from his bag a blood stained knife and 20,000 rubles very founded. Alesionov was not a convict, he was innocent but the proof were against him and he was sentenced to be flogged and sentenced to26 years of jail.

Aksionov 's life was charged in the jail. From a cheerful person he became very serious man. He passed 26 years in the jail.

One day a new convict named Makar semyonich came there. With his conversation Aksionov found our that semyonich was the real murdered of the merchant and for that he was passing his life in jail. Aksionov was very eager to take revenge on him. It was because of Makar he was living miserable life and separated from his dear wife and children. But when he meditated, he overcame his anger because he was not God. It was his fate that he was passing his life in jail. He did not have any right to give any justice when God was there. He realized that God was merciful and he would certainly gave him justice.

Makar semyonich was digging up the tunnel to escape from the jail. Aksionov founder saw that yet he did not reveal the truth when the prison authority asked him. God had given him the chance, to take revenge on his enemy, God wants to tempt him but he did not disclose the name of Semyonich. Aksionov could have taken revenge by getting semyonich arrested but he knew that "Forgiveness is the best form of Revenge". This noble act of Aksionov also changed the heart of Makar and he confessed his crime and the order of Aksionov's release came but Aksionov was no more alive in this world to meet his family.

The story illustrate the value of love kindness, goodness in the life of a man. The writer wants to emphasizes that every sinner can be referred. If he is treated with love and sympathy he would definitely improve. Aksionov is kindness suggests that virtue or nobleness produces virtue. Just as vices produce vice. Aksionov 's goodness reform the heart of Makar. Aksiovov knows that revenge is ineffective and wrong love for sympathy and consideration are needed to reform a bad man. Makar is deeply affected by Aksoonov is generous and noble behavior. His cruelty was faced with grate fullness. It is really said "that forgiveness works like a lotion on revenge. James Russell Lowell, writes in his poem "yussof" As one lamp lights another, no growsless so nobleness enkindled nobleness" Really, forgiveness or nobleness can change the mind of a person and inspire the man and this toy story very well present this moral.

(2) Justify the title of the story. "God sees the truth but waits "

God sees the truth, but waits" is an appropriate and suggestive title. Aksionov 's condition and suffering his faith in God. Truly justify.

Aksionov, the major character of the story was arrested for murdering another merchant with whom he had stayed in the inn. Aksionov was innocent. He had not murdered the merchant yet he was sentenced for 26 years of imprisonment. He could not prove himself innocent because from his bag a blood stained knife and 20,000 rubles were founded. His wife also suspected him she also believed that her husband might have murdered. If was shocking for Aksionov . He had never expected that his family members would believe that he was culprit.

Yet he was not discouraged he had faith in God. God would never give punishment to innocent. He said that "If seemed that only God could know thetruth, If was to him alone he must appeal and from Him alone expect mercy". If was enough for him that in the eyes of God he was innocent and God knew everything. He should not pray to any king but only to God who would give him justice. It was God wish that he was sentenced for 26 years of imprisonment and God would release him. His faith in God made him to forget his sufferings.

Leo Tolstoy wants to suggests that even God also test the man by sending many temptations. Aksionov was also tempted. He found out that Makar was the real murdered and he wanted to take revenge but he overcomes his anger by remembering God and his grace. Even he did not disclose the fact that Makar had dug up the tanned to the governor and saved him because God would certainly the vices and crimes. The virtues and goodness of man were always rewarded by God. Aksionov kindness changed the heart of maker and he confessed this crime and asked for forgiveness from Aksionov and Aksionov only said that God would forgive you" If we have committed any crime the God give us punishment or forgiveness. Only God has that power.

The story suggests that goodness, self sacrificing nature of Aksionov are tempted by God. In this world God always sends sufferings to good people and try to change their attitude, belief towards God. But a person like Aksionov never changes their faith in God. Even the suffering of prison does not shake his faith in God. He never blames or condemns God for his sufferings and pains. On the contrary he believes that it is his desting and God's will that he as passing his life in jail. Although at the end of the story he dies but with the satisfaction and peace of mind because maker confesses the crime and he proves innocent.

SWEETS FOR ANGELS

- **R.K. Naryan**

SUMMARY

Sweets for Angels is a touching story by famous Indian writer R.K.Narayan. The story presents one poor porter's love for children and his bitter experience.

Kali is the main character of the story. The story revolves round him his love for the school going children and one bitter experience make him to take a vow that he will never love them.

Kali was an orphan. He was living in Royapurum with his two friends named Kuppan and Pachai. Kali was a porter and likewise his two friends were also poor. Kuppan was a rickshaw driver but he was idle. Pachai begged at bus stands, as a 'blind man'. Although he was not blind. Kali was six feel tall and very strong. He looked frightening because of his beard and structure. All the day Kali dragged the bags of rice from a lorry to grain store. He was happy with such kind of life. He needed only one rupee for a day and that he could earn easily. He never lamented over his diving. (life).

Kali loved the school going little children. His heart filled with pleasure when he saw them. He looked at them with wonder and used to praise their ability to read and write. He worshipped them as holy angels But the children were not familiar about his love for them. He secretly watched them behind the school gate and the humming coming from the school filled his mind with "mystic Joy".

Kali one day earned much money than usual. He decided that he would not reveal it to his friends because they would inspire him to spend it. As his pocket was filled with money he went to the hotel and sat on the chair and drank two cups of coffee. He heard the school bell and he decided to go back to his place so that he could see the angels, the children. He saw different kinds of sweets and he bought it. He ate one piece of it and tempts to eat another but he remembered that these were for the children.

The children were coming. He held out the package towards three children but they were absorbed in their talk and did not give response to him. He also felt ashamed in the presence of these Angels. He offered sweets to another girl and boy. They were tempted by the sweet smell and color of the sweets. They hesitated but Kali's persuasion made them to accept the sweets. Very soon the children arrived and surrounded Kali. They started shouting and scrambling. Kali as well as the children were happy. The passersby were amazed by this commotion. When they knew that one man was distributing sweets, they moved towards kali. They caught kali and started shorting that "Help" Help" Here was the kidnapper of children." The people gathered and they suspected kali as the kidnapper of children because during those days five children were missing from the school and ten children had died because of poisoned sweets. And kali was seen giving sweets to the children. People misunderstood him ad started saying that "he was from monstrous sect, and every member of which had to surface a hundred children." Kali's appearance also made them believe that he was a kidnapper. Kali could not understand the reaction of the people. The crowd chased him. Kali ran but people beat him and he was wounded. Blood stickled down. He realized that his life was in danger and he got up and he ran and hide in house. The members of the house came out frighteningly. Kali lie down on the floor.

He was unable to move because he was tired and wounded. People were shouting outside and he became unconscious. The people entered into the house through roof and carried him out. The police arrived and saved him from the mad crowd. Being wounded he was taken to the hospital. After two weeks when he recovered, he found his two friends beside his bed in a hospital. They advised him to come back to his old place because people would not recognize him since the police had shaved off his beard and his hair. They also suggested him to avoid the children. Kali's answer was shocking. A man who loved the children too much, turned against them. The story ends with Kali's answer "Hereafter I will turn and run as if a tiger chased me, if I see the tiniest ahead of me in a street."

This story presents kali's love for the children but society can not recognize his love. Being illiterate kali worshipped the school going children as an angels. He wants to share his feeling with them and to shower his love over them. He loves the children so much that instead of spending the money for himself he buys the sweets for the children. They also accept his sweet. Although his appearance is frightening but they are afraid of him because his eyes are twinkled with love, there is no touch of betrayal or cruelty. Any child wants love and they find it in kali. But the society become cruel towards him. The people do not give him opportunity to speaks and beat him mercilessly. This bitter experience makes him hater of children. The decision which he takes is shocking. It is very difficult for him to live apart from the angels. But the society treats him so harshly that he turns against children. Really the society is responsible for kali's views and the poor porter's life will become dull.

QUESTIONS & ANSWERS

(1) What contrast does the blind man in the story hold to kali?

Kali was poor orphan porter; He was illiterate so he worshipped the school going children. For him they were angels. His heart was filled with delight whenever he saw them. He often remarked to his friend pachai "How did these babies read so much". He always felt inferior to them. He thought that he was just a wooden dummies in this world who could not do anything in this world. He praised the ability of the children to write and to read confidently. He loved them so much that sometime he walked behind them and enjoyed the sweet humming of the school. He worshipped the school and also the children.

He wanted to shower his love over them and brought sweets for them. By distributing sweets he wanted to get love of the children. He regarded them as an angels because he knew that angel never made difference between rich and poor. Angel always became friend who loved him whether he was rich or poor. He was poor but his heart has full of love for children.

The children accepted his sweets and became happy but the public, the mob thought that Kali was a kidnapper of children. The crowd was mad and without giving any opportunity to Kali started beating him. The mob was violent and they chased Kali. At first kali did not understand what sin he had committed. But the mob wanted to kill him and he found an opportunity and went into one house. Yet the mob wounded Kali and he was saved by the arrival of the police. For two weeks he was in a hospital and he took vow before his friend that he would turn and ran as if a tiger chased him if he saw any tiniest tot ahead of him in a street."

Kali was so disillusioned that he became bitter towards the children. Kali was innocent and un experienced man. He had illusion that the world was like him. The children were innocent and accept Kali friendship but the mob; the worldly people could not recognize Kali is admiration. For them he was only a kidnapper, whose existence in the society was dangerous. The reaction of the mob was also proper if we think it in other way. Because kidnapper tempts children with sweets. Kali was true and his decision shocks the reader. Kali realized the truth that if again he would shower his love over children, his life would be in danger and anyone loves his life too much. Kali was not a philosopher that he would continue his love or a adoration for the children even after such a bad experience. For him his life is precious like any person than the love of children.

THE LAST LEAF

- O. Henry

O. Henry was an American writer whose short stories are known for wit, wordplay and clever twist endings. He wrote nearly 600 stories about life in America. O. Henry's short stories are known for their wit, wordplay, warm characterization, and surprise endings.

SUMMARY

The Last Leaf is one a of the popular stories in the world of English literature by the greatest story writer 'O' Henry. The last leaf depicts the story of an artisan who saves the life of an artist by sacrificing himself.

The title "The last leaf is suggestive and symbolic. The story is all about the leaves on the ivy vive. It is the last leaf which saves Johnsy and it as the same last leaf which takes away Behrman's life but makes him immortal.

Sue and Johnsy were friends. They lived in Greenwhich village. On the top of a three storied brick hose. Both of them had a common interest in art and other things and they started studio together.

In the month of November pneumonia broke out in that part of the city. Many people had become the victim of pneumonia. Johnsy also became a victim of this epidemic, On examining Johnsy doctor said that she was seriously ill and mentally she had given up the hope of survival. She had no desire to live and therefore it was difficult to cure her. The entire pharmacopoeia looked silly as she had no desire to line. No medicine would prove effective as she was pessimist and accepted her destiny. The doctor advice sues to build up her will power.

When Sue was drawing a picture for a magazine story in Johnsy's room, she heard a low sound. Jouhnsy was looking out the window and was counting backward twelve, eleven, ten and soon. On hearing her counting like this Sue asked her what was she doing. She informed that she was counting those. Leaves she told her that she would die with the fall of the last leaf. Sue was astonished informed her that it was just only her whim. Her fear was psychological so no medicine could cure her, she was sure that she would die with the fall of last leaf. Sue told her to stop thinking because doctor was hopeful about her health.

Sue went to ground floor to call Behrman for her model. He was a painter but a failure in art. Sixty year old Behrman had been trying for forty years to paint a master piece which he had not yet begun. He was hopeful that one day he paints a master piece. Sue told him about Johnsy's fear and her mental condition that how she was connecting the end of her life with the falling of the last leaf.

Behrman was also surprised and could not understand the relation between the falling of a leaf and the end of life. To Behrman Johnsy's fear was only the result of the weak mind. If once this fear was removed her life could be saved. Behrman wanted to save Johnsy's life.

During the night when all were sleeping Behrman took his brush and colour and painted the leaf on the brick wall. He did this work even though it was raining and the wind was blowing. Next day when Johnsy awoke, she found the last leaf. Inspite of the beating rain and winding the ivy leaf still cling to the wall. She feel that she would not die and felt happy. Her fear was removed. The last leaf did not fall because it was not a real leaf. Behrman painted the leaf in such a way that it looked like real leaf. They came to know on the next day that Behrman had died of pneumonia in the hospital. It was a very cold night and so Behrman became victim of pneumonia and died. The old Behrman had sanctified his life for Jahnsy. They felt that it was his masterpiece which saved Johnsy.

Thus the last leaf became very meaningful and symbolic in the story. It is the last leaf which saves Johnsy life. The last leaf is also a masterpiece of Behrman. It was painted for noble cause. The last leaf also falfills Behrman's ambition of painting masterpiece before his death. The last leaf makes Behrman a savior. So the title, The last leey is attractive appropriate and touching.

QUESTIONS & ANSWERS

(1) Does the story contain the so called O. Hery twist at the end? If so, how?

The last leaf' is the famous story by O' Henry, celebrated American short story writer whose stories have become popular in all lands. His stories are remarkable for their compact plots, ironical coincidences and unexpected twist at the end. The end of "The last leaf" is also excellent. The excellence of the story lies in its touching end. The end of the story is unexpected but convincing.

The end of the story is sudden, unexpected and surprising. It is touching it is the end that makes the story great. The end is conniving and suitable. It is the end of the story that pervades throughout the story.

(2) Discuss character of Behrman.

O Henry's last leaf is not popular only for its end but also for its characterization The story depicts three characters Sue, Johnsy and Behrman. But it is Behrman who makes the story worth reading. Behrman, is one of the unforgettable characters in world fiction.

Behrman was an old painter of 60 year who lived on the ground floor beneath Johnsy Sue and house. He had

Michelangelo's Moses beard, because he thought that he was a great painter and tried to look one with his beard. It was his ambition to paint masterpiece. Behrman had been trying for forty years to paint a master piece which he had not yet begun. He could not fulfill his desire. In other words he was a failure in art. He eared by painting ordinary things for commerce and advertising. He used to drink and talk about his masterpiece.

He became a model, a hermit miner for Sue's painting. He was an artist and could understand the heart of an artist. Sue informed him about Johnsy's fear-her belief that she would die with the fall of the last leaf. She had given up all the hope about her life. Behrman considered it as her fancy. He also thought that it was psychological fear. Once this fear was removed she would live. He decided to save her. He thought out a plan. On that night when everyone was sleeping Behrman came out of his house. It was cold night and the cool wind were blowing. Behrman looked at ivy vine. There was no last leaf. He then took his lantern a ladder brushes and colour. He painted the leaf in such a way that it looked real. Next day Johnsy saw the painted leaf and thought it was a real leaf and out of her psychological fear of death Her feaf disappeared and fell that he could live.

But Behrman himself became the victim of pneumonia because of that rainy night Two days of severe fever he died at last Johnsy and Sue knew about the death of Behrman. To their surprise they look at the leaf. They find it painted. They considered it as Behrman's masterpiece. The last leaf that he painted proved his real masterpiece because it saved Johnsy's life His masterpiece was invaluable. Behrman) The last leaf fulfilled Belrmans ambition of painting master piece and it was fulfilled in a great way.

So the character of Behrman appear very ordinary in the beginning of the story, just an old painter but in the end it becomes a touching character. He sacrificed his life for Johndy. He was an artist and so he understand other artist. For him Johnsy's life was more precious than his because she was a budding artist. Whereas he was old. But life is life whether a man is young or old and Behraman by sacrificing his life save Johnsys life. His supreme sacrifice wins our hearts becomes an unforgetabgle character of fiction.

(3) Discuss character of Sue.

Sue was an upcoming painter. She was a young girl from California. She met Johnsy in Greenwich and became her friend. She met her in one restaurant and found their tastes similar in art. So they started a studio.

During the winter season there was an epidemic of pneumonia and his friend Johnsy become victim of that. During Johnsy's willness get acquainted with her character. She looked after Johnsy very kindly. She provided encouragement went and hope to Johnsy when she thought that she would die with the fall of the last leaf.

(4) Discuss of character of Johnsy.

Johnsy was an upcoming painter she was a young girl form the city Maine. Johnsy was her pet name; her real name was Johnsy. She met Sue, another budding painter at Greenwich. They met in one restaurant and of and that they had similar taste in art and after things and together they started studio.

During the winter there was an epidemic of pneumonia and unfortunately Johnsy became the victim of the disease. She was in bed ridden condition. he became so weak that she gave up all the hopes of her survival. The doctor was hopeful about her survival but he could not cure her because mentally she had given up hope of survival. Her friend Sue tried to build will power but she could vote.

From her bed through the window she could see a vine on a wall Because of the autumn the leaves are falling one by one. A stage came when it was easy for her to count the leaves. With the falling of the leaves she became more weak and pale. Not only that but she believed that she would die with the fall of the last leaf. Her fear was psychological. No medicine could cure her. As such with the fall of the lat leaf she was sure to die.

Her friend Sue tried to convince her that there was no connection with her life and the falling leaves. But she was not successful in convincing her. When Behraman an old painter came to know about Johnsy's psychological fear he decided to save her.

If once this fear was removed. her life could be saved. In a rainy night Behraman painted the leaf which looked like real. Next day when Johnsy saw the leaf she became happy and her fear was removed. She desired to live and asked Sue to give the chicken broth.

Johnsy realized her guilt and said to sue" If was a sin to want to die." She realized that only God gives life and so he could take it back" It is not good to want to die. She regained her will power and said" Sue, some day I hope to paint the Bay of Naples." When she learnt that Behraman scarified his life to save her, she felt sorry and she agreed with Sue that last leaf was Behramens Masterpiece.

Johnsy is a pitiable but memorable character.

SUN AND MOON

- Katherine Mansfield

Katherine Mansfield is a writer of short stories and during her life time 5 volumes of her stories were published. She wrote under the pen name of Katherine Beauchamp she belonged to New Zealand. As a writer of stories, she followed in the footsteps of the Russian novelist and story writer Chekov, and French writer Maupassant so she started a new type of story which blended French and Russian influences. Unlike Dourly Richardson and Virginia woof that are autobiographical, Katherine studied life objectively. Some of her stories have the suiting of New Zeland life, which in other she presents the weariness, frustration of her English life.

SUMMARY

Sun and Moon are small children. They are brother and sister. They are full of imagination, innocent &frank. One day there is a concert in their house. Sothe whole day there is a big preparation. All are busy in their work. Sun and Moon move freely and they found a sort of joy watching everybody going here & there and doing some work. Even nurse had no time to take of these children.

In order to make arrangement of the party the furniture of the dining room was shifted. The piano is put in a corner. In the kitchen preparation for the party is going on. When the cook shows them ice pudding they are happy. The Dining room is decorated with red ribbons & bunches of roses. The nurse also changes the clothes of them and prepares them for the party. But the mother instructs the nurse to send them when the bell rang. They are specially dressed for the occasion. But they are more like show pieces they are brought down to dining room for a formality where they greet and meet the guests. They are taken to their bed room by the nurse. They slept for some time. But then sun hears load noise & wakes up. Both of them sat on the top step. They watch the elder people who are enjoying it. Again they go to bed fall asleep but wake up by their father's voice. They go down and surprised to find the scene. The ribbons & roses were all untied. The red napkin on the table lay on the floor. The plates were dirty. The food was thrown about. The fruits peels were found here & there. They are disappointed and failed to understand what had happened. But the father pretends as if nothing had happened. The place is in a complete disorder. The people have enjoyed it whereas they are not allowed to enjoy the fun on the occasion.

"Sun and Moon", a touching story written by Katherine Mansfield presents the feelings and emotions of little children named sun& Moon The story is psychological study of little children's mind.

A concert is arranged by the parents of sun and Moon. For this there is a lot of preparation in the house. Like other children they also get a sort pleasure when they see the different things coming to their home. They take a childlike interest in the preparation. Their mother is busy preparing for the evening concert. She runs around the house the whole day, ordering things and looking after the whole arrangement she even does not have time to talk with her children and sun and Moon do not wish to disturb their mother. They are curiously watching the preparations

First the golden chairs arrived in the afternoon. After this flower pots came. They carried by men. When Moon saw these pots from the baloney she thought men were wearing hats on their heads. She was so little that she did not know the difference between real things & not real ones. As all are very busy in their work sun and Moon moved freely here & there. They found a sort of joy watching everybody going here and there and doing some work.

In order to make arrangement of the party, the furniture of the dining room shifted. The piano was put in a corner and corners are decorated with of row of flower Plot. Golden chairs are arranged. Sun saw a white faced man was doing something with piano. Again when they came they found red lights everywhere there were red ribbons & bunches of roses in the corners. In the middle they saw a little lake with rose petals floating on it.

In the kitchen also special dishes were cooked. Minnie, the cook was busy in preparing dishes but without tiredness, with laugh she was doing her work. She was helping a man who was making blancmange. Other cook was decorating the dish of fish. He sprinkled it with red, green and yellow bits. The dishes were arranged with almond and tiny round biscuits. But the most attractive thing was ice pudding which the children found in the refrigerator. It was in the shape of little pink house. There was snow on its roof, green window, brown door with a nut for a handle Moon can't resist to touch the roof of the hose.

The children were dressed specially for occasion. Sun put on a white shirt which had red & white daises speckled on it. He put on breeches & white socks Moon also put on dress. Sun was dressed in his Russian costume and Moon was dressed like a little angel. Both of them were happy with the hope that they would enjoy grand party with fullest joy.

Indeed, the preparations for the party were done with due care and the preparation for the concert was big and grand. Sun and Moon are eager to enjoy the concert sewing the preparation.

QUESTIONS & ANSWERS

(1) Discuss contrast between Sun and Moon

Katherine Mansfield's story "Sun and Moon" is an interesting story for the characters f little children Sun and Moon whose observation of the (party) preparation for the party and their reaction to it provides the reader to understand the psychology or the working of little mind.

Sun and Moon are brother and sister, They are little but Sun, the brother is elder to Moon and so somewhat mature, whereas Moon, the sister she appears childlike. The authoress very delicately presents the sensitive perception of these little children.

A concert is arranged in the house and for this lot of preparation is going on in the house. Both the children get pleasure by seeing it Moon is so little that she can't understand the difference between real things & not real as she mistaken the flower pots carrying by the people as hat.

The story presents the society of upper class, so the parents of these little children likewise busy with their work instead of paying attention to them. The mother of them is so busy in the preparation, in her dressing that she does not want any disturbance from her children and asks them (nurse) Out of my way children". Sun felt insulted and decided not to disturb her. He doesn't like his mother's order to (keep) be in their nursery whereas Moon doesn't care all-out Sun can understand that his mother's care more for her party than the feelings of her children Moon is so childlike that she can't resist to touch the ice pudding., but Sun just admire it In the party when sun is walking by holding Moon's hand. he does like it as he wants to walk alone & that is also with proud. In the party also Sun develops liking for one fat man who appears friendly with him. For Moon everyone is same & mixes with them.

The character of sun is more reflected in the end of the story. He is shocked by the condition of the dining room. Everything is in a disorder The roster, ribbons, napkins, glasses, plates, food & fruits. He cannot understand the behavior of the elders. He is so much shocked that he crys out " its horrid, horrid – horrid" and denies to eat the ice pudding. The parents are unable to understand the reason of his sadness and sends him to his nursery. Whereas Moon is eating the ice pudding.

Thus, Sun is little boy but gifted with emotions & Sensitivity and imagination. Even in his small age he has developed maturity but his parents are unable to share his feelings. The End of Sun and Moon, a touching story by Katherine Mansfield is enjoyable as it employs the technique of story writing perfectly. The success of any story lies in the presentation of its end which is sometime shocking or surprising. The end of the sun and Moon move heart of the readers as it is in contrast with the beginning of the story

The story begins with a description of the grand preparation for the concert in the house of sun and Moon the little children.

They curiously watch the preparation which is going on in the dining Room and kitchen. watching the preparation, they are eager to enjoy it fully with fun. The children are dressed up in their best clothes. But their mother instructed the nurse to bring them in the party for short period. They are dismayed somewhat. They are brought there as show pieces just for a formality of greeting the guests. Then they are sent away to their nursery. The older people enjoy the music food and company of one another. But Sun and Moon are kept away all along. They try to sleep but can't so they watch the party by sitting on the top steps. When the party is over they are allow to come (down) in the dinning room.

Sun is shocked by seeing the disorder of the room, Moon being little, eats the ice-pudding offered by her father. But Sun can't understand the behavior of the elderly people. The ribbons and bunches of rose flowers untied are were there on the floor. The dishes are dirty and on the floor bones, fruit peels are thrown. The emotional and sensitive mind of sun gets shock and he cries out "horrid". He is lover of beauty, order and tidiness but he is disillusioned by elderly people who must have enjoyed the party. It is an irony that the elders enjoyed everything at the cost of the children's joy. Sun starts shobbing but instead of consoling him or knowing the reason of his subbing his father Says" off with you" This behaviours of Sun's father reveals the nature of the people of upper-class who are unable to understand the feeling and emotions of their children.

The end of the story reflect satire on the parents of higher class who provides luxury to their children but unable to share their feelings and psychological needs of the children just as the parents of sun and Moon prevent them from enjoying the party and unable to understand the feeling of Sun. The disorder of the room also suggests (that) the way of enjoying the party by the elders which is hated by Sun who loves beauty & order.

Thus, Katherine Mansfield, by presenting an ironical end nicely present the state mind of little children through Sun and the world of elderly people.

A DAY'S WAIT

- Ernest Miller Hemingway

Ernest Hemingway (1898-1961) an American novelist occupies an eminent place in the history of English lit. He became a reporter and in the 1st world war he served in the Red cross with the Italian army. Hemingway produced most of his work between the mid-1920s and the mid-1950s, and won the Nobel Prize in Literature in 1954. He published seven novels, six short story collections, and two non-fiction works. Additional works, including three novels, four short story collections, and three non-fiction works, were published posthumously.

SUMMARY

A Day's Wait by Ernest Hemingway is an interesting story. The story presents the nine year old boy Schatz as the central character who is suffering from flu but develops an illusion that he is going to die. The story presents the tension felt by the little boy Schatz and through his tense mood Hemingway nicely depict the reality of life that no one can enjoy the life if he knows that he will die soon.

Schatz is a little boy of nine years. He becomes ill and complains about headache. His father advises him to take a rest but he continuously replies No, I am all right". It shows that he is feeling very much normal before the arrival of the doctor and neglects his illness. He does not take it seriously and appears to be normal.

But a change comes over to him when he is diagnosed by the doctor. His illness is diagnosed as mild flu. The doctor prescribes three medicines for him. One for bringing down the fever another for acidity and the third purgative the doctor says the boy is running 102^0 temperature. It means that he is not in a serious condition the medicines will certainly cure him. But being a little boy he misinterpreted the situation. He finds himself in a critical condition. He misunderstands the reading of the thermometer. Scathe is familiar with only Celsius and does not know anything about the Fahrenheit thermometer which is used by the doctors. At school he has learnt only about Celsius, which taught him that one cannot live with a temperature of 44 degree. Celsius and at 100 degree Celsius water starts boiling whereas he has 102 degree temperature. He is confused and develops an illusion that he is going to die soon as he misunderstands the reading of the thermometer. He does not know that on the Fahrenheit scale, the normal body temperature is 98 degrees and on the Celsius scale, it is 37 degrees.

So his ignorance about the Fahrenheit & Celsius scales of thermometer makes, him tense. Suddenly he loses his interest in life and tries to be detached from the world. His father tries to make him cheerful by reading aloud. Howard pyres "Book of

Pirates' but he does not seem to enjoy it as he has lost interest in everything. He has taken the medicines and when his father asks him "How do you feel yet he replies" Just the same so far' as he has that illusion that medicine cannot cure him. He also neglects his father's advice for sleeping and philosophically re;ies I had rather stay awake" as if he is sure that he will die soon. But the most touching thing about him is that he is brave He tries to be cool and asks his father to leave him alone He doesn't shed tears but bravely waits for his death. Next day his father finds him in the same position. He even doesn't allow his father to entre into his room because he believes that his father will also get the infection of flue Now he is totally become a psychological patient and his fear is also psychological Has fever is subsided so his future again give him the medicines but he denies by saying" Do you things it will do any good?" By this time he is so much upset that at last he asks his father "About what time do you think I have going to die. For his fear of death he states that he has 102 degree temperature.

The father realizes that his boy has misunderstood the reading of the thermometer. He convinces him that he is very much normal and tells him about the Fahrenheit and Celsius scale. His father also gives him a comparative idea of miles and kilometers. He clears his misunderstanding. Schatz, after realizing his mistake, slowly relaxed and his fear of death lessened. The next day he is very joyful and happy. So he is relieved of his fear of death and so also the readers. The misunderstanding about the reading of thermometer is the centre of the story.

Through Schatz's fear f death Hemingway highlighted the serious issue of life. We are so much absorbed in life that we forget that we have to leave this world but the reality of life is death and no one can escape from it. It is true that with our birth our day for death is also fixed but we ignore it and it is also good because a man cannot enjoy any happiness if he knows that he is going to die. The fear of death takes away all charms of life. So Gray rightly said "If ignorance is bliss.

It's folly to be wise" And schmaltz's character illustrates this.

THE GOLDEN TOUCH

- Nathaniel Hawthorne

Nathaniel Hawthorne was a 19th century American novelist and short story writer. He is seen as a key figure in the development of American literature for his tales of the nation's colonial history. Much of Hawthorne's writing centers around New England and many feature moral allegories with a Puritan inspiration. His work is considered part of the Romantic movement and includes novels, short stories, and a biography of his friend, the United States President Franklin Pierce

SUMMARY

The Golden Touch by Mr. Nathaniel Hawthorne, the famous American novelist list is a story dealing with the note of didacticism that wealth is not the soul of life. It is illustrated through the pight of king Midas lust for gold and his plight.

Excessive desire for wealth very of ten leads to discontent and misery and it is artistically represented by the author through the main character of the story king. Midas haw thorne has given modern touch to the ancient Greek myth of kind Midas. He was legendary king of Phrygia and he had a little daughter named Marygold. He was rich yet he was mad after gold wealth. But of course, he loved his little daughter more than gold. His lust for gold was so intense that he wanted to change the natural course of the universe as by watching the golden light of the sun at evening he used to wish that it could turn everything into real gold. He used to wish by seeing yellow flowers, that if they were as golden as they look, In his youth, he was lover of music but now he loved only the sound of gold coins. His lust for gold became so intense that he (wish) did not like to touch the normal things which were of not gold.

He kept his hard earned gold secretly in the cellar and used to count his gold pieces. Once, he was in his treasure house and wonderful fling happened. In his secrete measure room, he found a stranger and he at once realized that this stranger was nor ordinary man but a celestial being.

The stranger, looking at the treasure asked the king that he seemed to be very rich and king Midas replied that it had taken a long time to collect the gold but he lamented that if he could live a thousand years, he might have time to be richer. Observing him unsatisfied the stranger asked him what else he wants? and king Midas said "I wish everything I touch could be turned into gold." He asked for" the Golden Touch" and a boon was granted to him that tomorrow row at sunrise he would get Golden Touch.

This boon of 'Golden Touch" will bring disillusionment and it is presented that when in the early morning he found the things as it was in his room. He was disappointed that the boon was mot working. But with the first sunbeam of the rising sun as soon as he (touched) removed the bed sheet it had become cloth of gold. He was overjoyed with the advantage of the boon and as he touched the leg of the bed, curtain clothes, spectacles, all turned gold.

But he realized futility the of the boon when he sat for the breakfast. As he touched the coffee pot, egg, fish, the bread & butter, all turned into gold and he lamented "such costly food is before me and I can eat nothing". The daughter realized that something was wrong with her father and she came near to the king. King Midas Kissed her but to his surprise the daughter changed into a figure of solid gold. He realized that he was the poorest man in all the world if he did not have his daughter. The stranger again appeared to him and the king regretted that he had lost everything which he really loved. The stranger asked what was important Golden Touch or a cup of cold water and a piece of bread and his little daughter. And the king confessed that in life water, meal & child are more important, valuable than gold. The stranger told him that he had become wiser as he realized that the common things of life, which are within everyone reach are more valuable than riches and he asked him to bath in the river to remove the boon and to the sprinkle the same water on the statue of his daughter. The king got his daughter back. The story presents that lust for gold. Generally it is believed that power, wealth, knowledge make a man the most happiest but it is merely an illusion. The craving for it only brings unhappiness as life needs common things. The basic things which run the life like water, corn, and love are more essential to make the life beautiful. These things are easily available to man in order to make life happy but in order to surpass the common humanity by achieving greatness through power or wealth usually brings disillusionment as power and wealth are not imp for the survival of life It can make life comfortable, but they are not life. and this message is excellently conveyed through king Midas' disillusionment with the boon of "The Golden Touch."

QUESTION AND ANSWER

(1) Discuss first meeting between Midas and the stranger.

The Golden Touch" is a touching story written by Nathaniel Hawthorne. The story represents the king Midas' greed for gold and its consequence.

King Midas was Wealthy king but he was not satisfied with his riches. He craved for gold in life and to collect gold as much as possible became the motto of his life. He had a little daughter named Marigold and he loved her like anything and in order to make her life comfortable he collected gold madly. His craving for gold became so deep that he wished that God should create the natural objects made up by gold.

He had gathered all his precious gold in his secret treasure room and he used to count his gold pieces and he used to admirer his gold cups, plates and felt happy. Once he was in his treasure room and he was visited by stranger and he realized that this stranger must be divine being. Looking at the gold pieces in the treasure room the stranger asked "You seem to be a very rich man" And the king replied that after a struggle of long time he had collected. This gold and he wished that if God permitted him to live for a thousand years he would get time to get richer. The answer signifies that he was not content at all with his wealth and wished to live long in order to collect more wealth and thereby to become the immortal. The stranger recognized his unsatisfaction in life and asked what else do you wants? This question made the king to utilize the situation and his magical power and he replied that he was tired of collecting gold so slowly and said" I wish everything I touch could be turned into gold." He asked for the boon of "The Golden Touch". Before granting the boon the stranger asked him that would he never regret for it and king Midas thought how one could regret for such a precious boon It would give him perfect happiness not aware that it would make him the most unhappy man He was thinking only that with the help of the golden touch, he would have treasure of gold in comparison of other man. The stranger granted him the boon that Tomorrow at sunrise you will find that you have the gold. Touch-Thusking

Midas craving for gold appeared to him to be fulfilled by the meeting of the stranger and expected to become the richest man with the help of the boon of the golden Touch and little suspected that it would bring only sorrow in his life. The stranger's boon becomes means to him to be rich.

(2) How did Midas regain normally in life ?

"The Golden Touch" is a story reflecting the message that excessive desire for wealth very often lead to discontent and misery.'

The story presents kind Midas' greed for gold and his realization of a normal life. The king was lover of gold and developed passion of collecting gold. He had collected gold pieces in his treasure house. Once when he was in his treasure house a stranger visited him and granted him the boon that whatever he touched would change into gold. The king Midas was overjoyed by receiving the boon, little aware about its consequences.

The next at the early morning the boon started working and his bed sheet, leg of bed the captainships clothes were Horned into gold as soon as he touched them. He was happy with its fruitfulness But he realized its futility during his breakfast. He could not drink coffee, or ate egg. bread & butter, the as it also turned into gold with his touch and he realized the weakness of his personality. He lamented that costly meal was before me, and I could not eat. When his daughter Mary gold came to comfort him he touched her and she too changed into gold statue. He felt as if he was the poor man in the world as he lost his only loving daughter.

The stranger appeared again to him and he confessed the uselessness of gold in contrast with the valuable things like food, water in life the means of survival of life. He realised the futility of life without his daughter. The daughters was now lorded with gold, but it read no life and soul. He realized that commend things which are essential for the existence of life are more valuable than the gold & power. This realization made him wiser man and the stranger asked him to bath in the river in order to remove the boon of the Golden Touch. As he bathed in the river he felt as if the Wight had been lifted from his heart & body symbolically the lust for gold from his heart vanished and he felt free and became normal human being who was content with the creation of the god. He sprinkled the same water on the statue of his daughter and she also got her farmer shape. Thus when the king Midas overcome the weakness lust for gold he was able to regain his normal peace of mind and contentment.

THE TIGER IN THE TUNNEL

- **Ruskin Bond**

Bond is an Indian author of British origin. He is known for his contributions to children's literature.Ruskin Bond has now been writing for more than 5 decades. He has stressed more on the local elements of Himalayas in his writings. His writing style is distinct in a way that it tries to make reader understand the landscape and ethos through carefully mastered words.

SUMMARY

The Tiger in the tunnel, by Ruskin Bond is a story, reflecting bravery of Baldeo and His son Tembu.

Baldeo, a tribal man was a watchman at the station in the forest. His duty was to give signal to the approaching mail train and to see that the lamp should burn during the night. His family was small consisting of his son Tembu, daughter and his wife. They lived in a small tribal village on the out skills of the forest. He owned small rice field but he did not earn much so he considered that he was lucky to get a job as a wachman at the station.

The story opens with the scene of midnight, when Baldeo prepared himself for his night duty. The station was three miles away from his hut and he was walking towards the station, he loneliness of night reminded him of the wild animal he might encounter in the forest as villagers were talking of the man-eater tiger and the panthers, though Baldeo had never seen them. But he maintained his self confidence as he thought about his axe. It was small and fragile but became deadly when it is used, it was a permanent companion of Baldeo, whether he went to tribal dance, or market. It was made by his father he even killed a young boar with it. He loved his axe dearly so even it was demanded by one official at big rate he didn't accept the offer.

On reading to the station, he gave the signal, checked the tunnel and lighted the lamp and waited for arrival of the train. But it was late and he started dozing suddenly the grunt of tiger woke him up and before he could decide anything it stood before him. Baldeo, becoming brave, without fear with his axe got ready for the fight with the tiger and saved himself from the paw of the tiger with axe he wounded the tiger on the shoulders but unluckily it stuck to its shoulder he was left without weapon. The angry tiger, with al its strength sprang upon Baldeo and tore him Baldeo died bravely. His tragic death arouses the feeling of pathos. The tiger was also wounded and the approaching train also killed him in it two pieces.

The true pathos lies at the and of the story Baldeo's son Tembu lamented over the untimely death of his father for two days. But life must go on suddenly Tembu, a small boy of 11 years become mature, tried to take up the responsibility of the family. And he tries to forget the death of his father and accepted the job of his father as a watchman. The end of story shows him at the station in the midnight he was waiting for the arrived of the train without any fear. Being the only male in the clamily, Tambu at a small age becomes the head of the family and tries to fulfill the duties of his father. The job of his father was risky as he had to give up his life Tambu was aware about the dangers attached to this job but accepted the job to earn the livelihood for the family. This maturity at the small age shows the pathos that his childhood has been snatched away from by the untimely death of his father. But he was feeling proud that his father had killed the tiger and now he owned the axe of his father. Thus, the whole story is full of pathos. The fight between Baldeo and tiger and the tragic death of Baldeo and the condition of Tembu arouse the feeling of pathos and the hearts are moved.

QUESTIONS & ANSWERS

(1) Describe the encounter between Baldeo and the Tiger.

The Tiger in the tunnel, is a tragic story but it exhibits the courageous nature of its main character Baldeo. The story is enjoyable due to the scene of the encounter between Baldeo and the tiger in the forest.

Baldeo was a watchman at the station. He was a tribal man. Every night he had to go for the duty at night on the station which was in the forest. The villagers talked of the wild animals like the tiger and panthers in the forest but Baldeo did not feel afraid as he kept his axe with him, which was small & fragile but deadly when it was used.

Once Baldeo was performing his duty at night and waited for the arrival of the train. It was late so he felt steeply but suddenly he woke up by hearing the grant of the tiger from the top of the cutting. He became alert and guessed whether her it would go in the direction of his hut where his wife & son Tembu were sleeping unprotected. But before he could make out its direction he found the huge tiger trotting towards him. He could not run as the tiger could see clearly during the night. So he decided to stand before it. The tiger knew how to kill its prey. So came on fearlessly and with its right paw attacked on Baldeo.

Baldeo, was also prepared with his axe and he avoided its paw & wounded the tiger's shoulder with his axe. The tiger became angry and again came near to him and Baldeo this time raised his axe to wound the tiger on definite aim, but the axe got stuck in the bone and Baldeo was left without any weapon. The tiger was severely wounded but now if become easy for him to kill Baldeo and he brought him down Baldeo was killed by the tiger.

The whole scene exhibits the bravery of Baldeo. He bravely faces the attack of the tiger and also wounded it with his dear axe and bravely faces his death.

(2) Discuss theme of the Story

The tiger in the tunnel is a story which (presents) not only present the courageous nature of Baldeo but also the theme that life must go on Death cannot steal the charm of life. It is reflected through Tembu, the son of Baldeo.

Bldeo, a watchman was killed by the tiger when he was on his night duty at the forest the fought bravely against the tiger and died. So his character reflects the physical strength of human being. Tembu, his son wife and sister lamented over the death of Baldeo. Tembu exhibits the moral strength as he guarded the dead body of his father at the forest in the darkness of the night. On that very moment from 12 years of age he become mature. The death of his father shocks him but he maintained his confidence and tolerated the sudden tragic death of his father.

After three day he became normal as the end of the story shows him on the place of his father, giving lighting the signal lamp for the mail Life has to go on and a living had to make. Death is the reality of life. It comes sooner or later to everyone and this reality Tembu has accepted. It is useless tomorrow for long time on his father's death. He is now the head of the family. He has to look after his mother and sister. The responsibility to earn livelihood for them now fell on Temble for which he should come out of the grief. The only means of their live hood was to accept the job of his father as a watchman, which was risky and the sad memories are attached to it. But Temba like his father reflects the moral strength and started working as a watchman. He developed positive attitude that the gods of the forest were happy as his father had killed the man eater tiger. Beside he now inherited the axe of his father, and he know how to use it when required. So without any fear Tembu started his career as a watchman.

Thus the writer through Tambu's life after his father's death shows that life on earth never stops. Time is the best remedy and man accept the reality of death cheerfully, that it can never snatch away the existence of life from the earth. The death can never crush the spirit of man to live on this earth. So Hemingway rightly said" Man can be destroyed, but cannot be defeated?

MR. KNOW ALL

- **Somerset Maugham**

William Somerset Maugham was a British playwright, novelist and short story writer. He was among the most popular writers of his era and reputedly the highest paid author during the 1930s. During and after the war, he travelled in India and Southeast Asia; all of these experiences were reflected in later short stories and novels.

SUMMARY

"Mr. Known All" is an interesting story by Somerset Maugham, Who is a Versatile Writer of the modern age. The Present story depicts Maugham's art of Characterization. The whole story revolves round the character of Mr. Max Kelada, who is the center of interest for the readers. His character is presented through the Narrator of the story Who has a prejudicial dislike for Mr. Max Kelada.

The narrator had to accompany him for 14 days journey in a liner. Mr. Max Kelada was a Levantine whereas the narrower was an English man So before meeting him personally the narrators started a feeling of dislike for him. And as he met- him personally his disliking for Max Kelada increase due to the natures of max. Kelada.

Max. Kelada was Short and of a sturdy build, Clean shaven with hooked nose. He used to makes excessive use of gestures. He was talkative man and his discussion includes plays, Picture and politics. He had a mixing nature so that he could address any one without putting "Mister" before the name and only in their days he became familiar with everyone on the ship. He took leadership in all the competitions of sport, Concerts and fancy dress ball. Because of his talktive nature and boatful nature he was hated by all. As he assumed that the knewn everything better than anybody else. He possessed a good Skill of argumentation and so he would not drop the subject, till he convinced the listener with his way of thinking. He was confident and that he couldn't believe that he might commit any mistake. He always talked with the people whether they like or not or want his company or not. According to the narrator he was the best-hated man in the ship. They use to call him ironically "Mr. Known all" but he used to take it as a compliment half of the story then present Max. Kelada's character artistically. The narrators repeated comment about- Max Kelada that " I did not like Mr. Kalada " intensify the hatred of narrator for Mr. Kalada and with him we also develop a feeling of dislike for him.

But the later part of the story puts him on a high esteem. The incident of the Bet between Mr. Kelada and Mr. Ramsay throws more light on Mr. Kelada is true nature. Mr. Kelada was doing the business of the pearls and for one of his business transactions he was going to Japan one day the discussion on the dining table turned to pearls and Mr. Kelada very confidentially said that he knew all the best pearl in the world and bet with Mr. Ramsay that the pearl chain of Mrs. Ramsay was real worth $30,000 where as Mr. Ramsay who was told by his wife that it was an imitation worth $ 18, got read to bet him $ 100 that it was imitation. Mr. Kelada examined it closely and found it to be real. He was about to declare but he saw suddenly a feeding of embarrassment in the eye of Mrs. Ramsay. He realized the critical situation of Mrs. Raursay and declared that Mr. Ramsay won the bet as the pearls were really imitated. Thus he lost the bet and also invited disgrace for him that he was a boastful man.

Thus the end nicely heightens the character of Mr. Kelada as he saves Mrs. Ramsay's dignity as a woman. The narrower also realizes the true nature of Mr. Kelada. His character reflects that generally we judge a personal outwardly through his behavior and appearance. But man is notwhat he seems. Mr. Kelada has an understanding heart as he saves Mrs. Rausay at the cost of his own disgrace. Outwardly he appears very talkive & boastful but he wins our heart and with the narrator we also change our opinion about Mr. Kelada and we really appreciate him as Mr. Know All."

QUESTION & ANSWER

(1) Discuss the end of the story.

Someerset Maugham has made the story. "Mr.Know All" more interesting by presenting surprising end though the incident of bet between Mr. Kelada & Mr. Ramsay Mr. Kelada was going to Yokohame in one liner. He was very talkative man and had a mixing nature. He tried to be familiar with everyone on the ship. His fellow passenger used to call him "Mr. Know All" as he assumed as if he knew everything – plays, pictures, politics all subjects of the world. He used to take his dinner with Mr. Ramsay, the doctor & the narratar of the story. On the table they always discussed. One evening at dinner the conversation by chance turned to the subject of pearls. Kelada, according to his habit rushed to the new topic. He told them all about the cultured & Real Pearl Here, he revealed that he was doing the business of pearls Mr. Ramsay started arguments and soon it turned into a heated discussion Mr. Kelada very confidentially declared that it was impossible to pass off under his nose a cultured pearl as a real one. He pointed to the chain of Mrs. Rausay and declared it to be real worth $ 30,000. Mr. Ramsay who was told by his wife that it was an initiation worth $18 only, got ready to bet him $ 100 that it was imitation.

Mr. Kelada who was dogmatic cheerfully accepted the bet as

he did not like to be challenged. He examined the chain with his magnifying glass and found it to be real. But the condition of Mrs. Ramsay was critical. She smiled with difficulty as she did not wish that her pearls be examined. But her husband was eager to earn easily money as he had complete faith in his wife and the price would not be wrong. He believed that every time Mr. Kelada couldn't be cocksure. Mr. Kelada was about to reveal it but suddenly he noticed a desperate appeal in the eye of Mrs. Ramsay. He, at once realized that she must have told wrong price to her husband as she must have got it as a gift from someone. He decided to close the bet and calmly gave $ 100 to Ramsay. He lost the won bet and also invited disgrace for himself to save the dignity of woman. But this behavior of Mr. Kelada makes him a real hero.

Indeed, the end of the story presents the true nature of the characters Mr Kelada who is disliked by the narrator, is able to win his heart and he finds a new trait of Mr. Kelada's personality as he tears the envelope and takes $ 100. He remarks that no one would like to be being made a fool in public. The narrator asked if the pearls were real he only replies that if he had a pretty little wife, he'd not let her be alone for a year in New York. It shows that Mr. Kelada has an understanding heart as well as ready to invite any disgrace if it would do-good to others. He is not what he appears. Thus, the end of the story really appears to be surprising.

MY LOST DOLLAR

- **Stephen Leacock**

SUMMARY

The writer has given one dollar to his friend Todd when he was going to Bermuda. He gave the dollar in change to pay rent of taxi, very naturally he gave it but though one year has passed yet, the friend has not given him back as he has forgotten it on several occasions the writer tries to remind him. When he came back from Bermuda after three weeks, on the platform out of courtesy the writer welcomed him. And in order to remind him of dollar he proposed to go in taxi But, the friend preferred to go by walk. Even during the evening the writer by asking him what currency issued at Bermuda, tried to remind him of his dollar, but it did not bring anything to Todd's mind. Thus, the writer felt that he had lost the dollar. But this realization bring one thought to the writer himself that just as Todd owes a dollar, and forgotten it must happen that the writer himself owes a dollar and also forget to repay it. There may the list of them. He wants to remember them in alphabetic order. He doesn't want to remember the names of men who had lent him 30 shillings. He wants to start a general movement Back to Honestly movement for paying all these odd dollar that are borrowed.

"My lost Dollar" by Stephen Leacock is an interesting essay written in humoures style, with didactism. Behind its light hearted treatment of the subject, the writer draws the attention on the general folly of human nature with which the writer himself is suffering also.

The narrator the writer had once given a dollar to his friend Mr. Todd. He borrowed the dollar when he was going to Bermuda and in order to pay a change to his taxi. The narrator had lent it very naturally but when it was not repaid after months, the narrator realized that he had lost his dollar. He felt that it would never be paid in future also as the friend had totally forgotten it. It didn't make any effect on their friendship but the narrator was unable to forget that Mr. Todd owed a dollar to him.

The narrator tried a lot to remind him about the dollar. When from Bermuda Todd sent him a letter, he expected a dollar inside the envelope but he was dismay when Mr. Todd returned from Bermuda, the narrator welcomed him at the station and proposed to go home in taxi, but his friend preferred walk and again the narrator was dismayed. During the evening, when they were talking about Bermuda the narrator asked him about the currency that was used at Bermuda, but again it could not remind. Mr. Todd about the borrowed dollar. Even the narrator asked him about the cost of his trip, but this reference again did not bring anything to Todds mind and the Narrator was completely convinced that Todd had really forgotten the dollar. The Narrator at last hopelessly included Todd in the list of men who owed a dollar from the narrator and had forgotten to repay it.

Once in the club his friend Todd made remark about Poland, that Poland would never pay her debts but he was not conscious about his own debt to the narrator, This behavior of Todd brought a painful thought to the narrators mind. He thought just as Todd had forgotten repay the dollar in the same manner, it was possible that he had borrowed a dollar from somewhere and forgotten to pay it.

Thus, behind the veneer of humorous treatment the writer tried to probe into his own conscience. He should not blame his friend for forgetting owed dollar because he might have forgotten the owed dollar to someone. Generally whenever we point out any shortcoming or folly to anyone we have to check whether we do not have the same folly. No one in the world exists without any weakness as we are all mortal beings. So before pointing any folly to other, one should peep into one's own self. The weakness in someone should remind you, your own weakness. It's really easy to find out a fault in someone, but its great to accept the same folly cheerfully in one's personality. The writer realizes this fact and his grudge against his friend gradually disappeared and he thought that not only one but from many he might have borrowed dollar and he wanted them to remind their names in alphabetical order. He also remembered that he did not want to remember these from whom he borrowed 30 cents He wanted to start Back to Honesty' movement, so that he could pay all those dollars.

This way this essay awakens not only the conscience of the narrator about common shortcoming but also ours and we inspired to overcome it.

What are Stephen.........

With what result......

"My lost dollar" is an essay with full of humorous elements. It arouses humour, as the narrator tries to recall his friend about the borrowed dollar but the friend has completely forgotten it.

The Narrators friend Mr. Todd owed a dollar. One year was passed yet Mr. Todd has not paid it. The narrator remembers that when his friend was going to Bermuda, in order to pay change to his taxi, he borrowed a dollar from the narrator and he gave it with a notion that he would pay it certainly. On several occasions The Narrower has tried to remind him but he fails. Their friendship remains intact but the narrator is unable to forget that his friend had borrowed a dollar.

When he wrote a letterform Bermuda the narrower enthusiastically opened it with a hope to get a dollar but he was disappointed. When Mr. Todd came back, he received him on the platform and in order to remind him about the boomed dollar he proposed to go home in taxi but the friend preferred walking Even in the evening by asking about the currency of Bermuda, the narrower brought the talk of American dollar but again he was dismayed. Even he asked about the cost of his trip, it did not bring anything to the mind of Todd and the narrator now realized that Todd has forgotten it and he had lost his dollar forever. One year has passed and now it does not appear that Todd will ever give it to the narrator.

EXERCISE

(1) Discuss the significance of title 'My Last Dollar'.

(2) Write down short note on Stephen Leacock

(3) Discuss the humour elements of My Last Dollar.